AN HISTORICAL SKETCH

OF

GOA

THE METROPOLIS OF THE PORTUGUESE SETTLEMENTS IN INDIA

With an Account of the Present state of the celebrated city, and of the surrounding Territories under its immediate Jurisdictoin, collected from the most authentic sources

DENIS L. COTTINEAU DE KLOGUEN

GYAN

Published by

GYAN

Gyan Publishing House
5, Ansari Road
Daryaganj, New Delhi-110002
Phone: 011-47034999, 9811692060
E-mail: books@gyanbooks.com

Distribution Network
gyanbooks.com
India, USA, Canada, UK, Australia, France

ISBN : 978-81-212-3497-9 (PB)
First Published, Madras, 1831

2nd Impression 2020

Printed at: Gyan Press, Delhi.

An Historical Sketch of Goa
Author: Denis L. Cottineau De Kloguen

AN HISTORICAL SKETCH
OF
GOA

AN HISTORICAL SKETCH

OF

GOA,

THE METROPOLIS OF THE PORTUGUESE SETTLEMENTS IN INDIA:

With an Account of the present state of that celebrated City, and of the surrounding Territories under its immediate Jurisdiction, collected from the most authentic sources,

AND

UNDERTAKEN AND DEDICATED

TO

HIS EXCELLENCY THE HONORABLE

MAJOR-GENERAL SIR JOHN MALCOLM

K. C. B. AND K. L. S.,

AND THE MEMBERS OF THE BOMBAY AUXILIARY OF THE ROYAL ASIATIC SOCIETY.

BY THE LATE

Reverend Denis L. Cottineau de Kloguen,

HONORARY MEMBER OF THE SAME SOCIETY, OF THE MADRAS LITERARY SOCIETY, AND OF THE PHILOTECHNICAL SOCIETY OF THE ISLAND OF BOURBON.

MADRAS:

Printed for the Proprietor by WILLIAM TWIGG

AT THE GAZETTE PRESS,

1831.

Cottineau's History of Goa

A RARE WORK LONG OUT OF PRINT

But now Republished

FOR A

Souvenir of the Exposition at Goa.

November-December 1910.

BOMBAY.

B. X. FURTADO & SONS.

1910.

Preface to this Edition.

The celebrations at Goa arranged for November-December 1910 have afforded a suitable opportunity of reproducing a small but admirable volume on Goa written by Pere Denis L. Cottineau de Kloguen, one time chaplain of Colaba, who spent a long time in Goa studying the history of the old city, and then wrote a book which deserves to be called a classic. It was published at Madras in 1831 just after the death of the author, with a map showing the actual state of the city of Goa at the very time he wrote—a state far different from now. For at his time the Religious Orders were still flourishing in the convents, their expulsion taking place only a few years later—*i. e.* in 1835; and many of the churches now totally disappeared, were then either intact or visible in their decay. With some omissions it was taken almost bodily by Fonseca into his *Historical Sketch of Goa*; and some of the parts omitted are just those which one would desire to have left in.

The text of this volume, having first been printed in the Examiner, is now issued as an Examiner Reprint —thus doing good service to librarians and students of ecclesiastical history, most of whom may never have come across Cottineau's treatise.

The whole Edition has been taken over with exclusive right of sale by Messrs. B. X. Furtado & Sons of Bombay, to whom therefore all orders should be addressed.

The text has been copied entire, and typed almost in the original form. The map has been reproduced photographically from the original, except that the explanations and references which surround it have been slightly modified in form and set up in type, for greater convenience. Readers should always bear in mind that all features of Goa as actually seen by the author refer to about the year 1827.

A Short Biographical Sketch of the Author.

THE Reverend DENIS LOUIS COTTINEAU DE KLOGUEN, was born in Nantes, a sea-port, S. W. of Paris, in France. In the early part of his life, he manifested a strong zeal for religion, and an entire devotion to its pious cause, which made him assume holy orders. Thinking, however, that his sphere of utility, in a country which teemed with persons of his profession, would be but very circumscribed, he resolved to go over to distant parts of the world, where his clerical labours might be more extensive, and where a larger field might offer itself for the exercise of those talents which he had received from the hands of nature; a great thirst after knowledge, and an acquaintance with the world, formed also two other ingredients in the compound of his resolution, to quit the land which saw him born, and wander on foreign soils. He accordingly left France, the place of his nativity, for England and America; and visited those countries. His stay, in the former of these places was not long, comparatively with his residence in the latter, where, he resided in the city of Baltimore, for the period of ten years. Here, he devoted himself to the duty of disseminating Christian knowledge among those of his brethren, who were roving in darkness and ignorance, as became a minister of the Gospel, and a faithful steward of the house of the Lord. In the year 1806, as teacher of Geography, he published his book entitled, *Geographical Compilation for the use of Schools*, in two volumes *duodecimo*; the utility of this work and the happy reception it met with, are evident, from the number and respectability of the many individuals who subscribed to the work, in Maryland, Washington City, George Town, Philadelphia, Lancaster, Carlisle, Pitsburgh, Hanover (in the county of York), New York, Brooklyn, Albany, Schenectady, Trenton, Burlington, Brunswick, Elizabeth Town, and Delaware. From America, the Rev. Mr. COTTINEAU returned to France, whither, the desire of seeing his mother, and of beholding once more the scene of his youthful engagements took him. He soon left France a second time, and proceeded to the isle of Bourbon; in which place he resided for several years, and was admitted a member of the Philotechnical Society. He afterwards set out for the island of Bombay, where he resided for a long while, and became one of the members of the Bombay Auxiliary of the Royal Asiatic Society. In this place he commenced and completed in French, his native language, an History of India, from the date of the Flood down to the year he lived; as also the present work on Goa. Shortly before his demise, he proceeded overland to Madras, with an intention of going thence to Calcutta, both which presidencies he was anxious to see before he should leave India and return to France for the last time, which it was in his contemplation to do; but, unfortunately, a constitution naturally weak, and broken down by the long voyages and laborious travels he performed, in countries, whose climates are so prejudicial to European health, cut the thread of life, and consigned him to a world of better existence; where, he is no doubt gone to receive the reward of a life well spent in the discharge of those duties, which devolved upon him as a man and a Christian. He died on the 11th February, 1830, at Karrical, a French Settlement, about 178 miles distant from Madras.

AN

HISTORICAL SKETCH OF GOA,

The Metropolis of the Portuguese Settlements in India, with an account of the present state of that celebrated City, and of the Territories under its immediate dependence.

THE city of Goa is famed throughout the world: few men are ignorant of its name, its geographical situation, and its title of capital of the Portuguese Asia. The part, which it took in the general transactions of the Portuguese in the East, its triple capture in 1510, the glory and wealth which it acquired soon after, and its decay, since nearly two centuries, are recorded in all the books that treat on those subjects; but its local history, the different sites which it occupied, its extent and population at the different periods of its splendour and decline, the state and number of its principal buildings, the time when they were erected, its diverse institutions and laws, the manners of its inhabitants, the different classes into which they are divided, are all very little known, or have been hitherto most erroneously represented. What is still less known is the actual extraordinary state of that famous city, and of the populous and important territories which surround it, to which it gives its name, and of which it is still the nominal capital. Few European travellers now visit Goa; generally when they do go to see it, they remain there but for a few hours, and as the English and Hindostany languages are very little spoken or understood in that place, the stranger is deprived of the means of information; add to this, its visitors confine themselves either to Goa, which is now rather a collection of churches and convents in the midst of a desert, than a real city; or to Pangi, which is a new and small town that has nothing absolutely remarkable in it; they never think of going to or of gathering informations concerning the provinces of Salsette and Bardes, which are far more populous and flourishing than the island of Goa, and constitute the residence of the most wealthy inhabitants. It follows from these facts, that all the modern accounts of Goa, given in the geographical treatises, must be and indeed are very unsatisfactory and very incorrect.

The writers tell you indeed, that it is very much decayed, but to what degree they mention not; they call Pangi *New Goa*, and Goa itself *Old Goa,* denominations unknown to the inhabitants, and which have been the source of very great mistakes; they seem to be ignorant that a population of half a million of souls, among whom are nearly 300,000 Christians, inhabit the surrounding territories, and still acknowledge the Portuguese domination. The state of Goa and the fluctuation it experienced in its wealth and population since three centuries, are likewise but very imperfectly known, as the old Portuguese books are rare and seldom read, and informations have been only gleaned from the short and very incomplete accounts given by the French travellers, Tavernier and Dellon, some Missionaries, and a few other obscure individuals. It is therefore to supply that deficiency, and to testify my gratitude for the honour which an illustrious Society has done me, in admitting me in the number of its members, that I have undertaken the present sketch, which, I humbly hope, will be acceptable and useful to all enlightened readers desirous of enlarging the sphere of their knowledge.

Goa was the first object of my observations upon my arrival in India. I resided for more than a month in the Archbishop's palace, conversing daily with that prelate on the history of his Metropolitan see; I daily visited the different edifices and monuments of the city and its suburbs. I repeatedly conversed with the principal members of the clergy and heads of the monasteries,—I had access to the various libraries, and even to the public records; and a remarkably well informed Governor of Daman, supplied me with those documents which circumstances prevented me from gathering myself. Although I cannot speak the Portuguese, I understand it as well as I do the English, from its analogy with the French, my native language, and with the Spanish which I learned in my infancy. I have taken care of course to consult the original Authors as much as possible, but unfortunately I found still much wanting in my researches. In the first place, the earthquake which destroyed Lisbon, having been the cause of the loss of many ancient books and records, orders were issued to have a great part of those extant in the colonies and chiefly in Goa, transported to Europe. Subsequent to this, the dark policy of the Marquis of Pombal, the Prime Minister of King Joseph, assisted by the misguided prelate whom he had raised to the See of Goa, despoiled anew the library of the Archbishopric of its most valuable books and manuscripts; and many of those that remain have been partially destroyed by those insects so prejudicial to books and libraries in India. I however think few interesting facts and circumstances relative to Goa have escaped my enquiries. I have carefully examined also, all that has been said on the subject by foreigners, and though I generally *found* in their writings much more to grieve than instruct me, I have endeavoured to separate the good grain from the tare, and truth from falsehood. Since I left Goa and returned to Bombay, I neglected no opportunity of reaping informations from the Portuguese residing in that Presidency. It is only after composing my notes from these very numerous and authentic sources, and after one year's meditation, that I have been emboldened to present the result of my researches to the public under the form of an historial sketch.

In order the better to elucidate the subject, and to render my account less tedious to the readers, I will divide it into several sections: The first shall exhibit an historical view of the origin of the town of Goa, its various revolutions, the fluctuation of its population, and the extent of its rising and declining state to the present day. In the second we will give a correct chronological list of its viceroys or governors, with the most remarkable events that took place in each administration. The third will set forth the chronology of its Bishops and Archbishops, its provincial councils, its religious institutions, the erection of its principal churches and other religious edifices ; and in this section, some thing will be necessarily said respecting the Jesuits and the inquisition, which may perhaps contradict what has been said heretofore by the generality of writers, but which has nevertheless appeared to me to be true and correct, after a most strict and impartial investigation. The fourth shall contain a faithful and accurate topographical description of the city of Goa in its present state, of the island on which it is situated, called also Goa or *Tissuary*, and of the old and new surrounding provinces on the main land, composing the actual government of Goa. The fifth and last will be confined to the population and present state of Society in the territories herein referred to, and the different circumstances of their colonization whereof that state is the result.

S. I.—Historical Sketch of the Town of Goa in general, from its origin to the present time--Its revolutions--Changes in its extent—Wealth, and Population —Its rise and decline, with the causes thereof.

WE find the first mention made of the name of Goa, in Ferishta's history of the Deccan, under the reign of Mujahid Shaw, the 3rd Emperor of the Bhamani dynasty, who began his reign in 1374. Goa is said to have been a seaport, appertaining then, as it did for near a century afterwards, to the Kings or Roys of Beejanuger. We know by traditon, transmitted by the natives to the first Portuguese settlers, that the Hindoo religion was then the only one professed in the island.

In 1469, according to the same author, Mullek ul Tijur Khaje Jehan, general Vizier and Prime Minister of Shumse or Mahomet II. the 13th Bhamani Emperor of the Deccan, took the island of Goa from Humrajee, regent of Beejanuger, who governed that kingdom during the minority of the sons of Severoy. The Deccanese monarch ordered great rejoicings on this occasion, and rendered the greatest honours to his Minister. At his request he gave the government of the new conquered place to Kishwer Khan, one of his officers who had distinguished himself in the conquest. Three years after, Perkna, Rajah of Belgoan, at the instigation of the regent of Beejanuger, came to retake Goa; but the Sultan of the Deccan marched in person in its defence, and having attacked Belgoan, forced the Rajah to return in order to defend his capital. In 1479, according to Antonio de Sousa, in his *Oriente Conquistado*, Miguel Oum, at the head of the Mahometans of Onor, persecuted by the Rajah of that place, who was tributary to Beejanuger, retired to Goa under the protection of the Deccanese Sovereign, who professed the same religion. It is then that Goa was built in its present place; for before that period, the town stood near two miles to the southward, about the centre of the island, and nearer to the southern shore. Of that first town there remain at present but some wretched hovels around the parochial church of St. Andrew, but the spot is still known by the appellation of Old Goa, which modern travellers have, of late, improperly applied to Goa itself. This new town, built by the Moors or Mahometans on the northern shore of the island, opposite to that of Divar, soon became a very flourishing place by the excellence of its harbour; but it was not very extensive, according to the Dutch traveller Linschoten, who tells us, that in 1583, when he arrived in Goa, the walls thereof were still standing, though the gates had been pulled down to facilitate the communication with the new built part of the city. He informs us that the walls of Goa, built by the Mahometans, were defended by a dry ditch, but he does not describe the exact extent of the ancient town; he only says that in his time it was twice larger. However, from what he and other travellers say, and from my own observation on the spot, I suppose that its length along the shore from East to West, was from the old custom house, the palace of the governor and the convent of St. Cajetan, to the small inlet that still separates Goa from the suburb of St. Peter or Pannely, including therefore not only the Arsenal but the College of St. Bonaventure which latter must have been built on the ruins of the ancient walls. Towards the South the Town must have been bound by the mountain of the Rosary, and the other rising ground back of the convent of *Bom-Jesus* and the present bazar. According to this supposition, which appears the most plausible, the city must have been hardly three-quarters of a mile in length, and not a quarter in breadth. Soon after the migration of the Moors, the empire of the Deccan having undergone a new division of government by the advice of Mulek ul Tijur, Goa fell to the lot of Fukhir-ul-Moolk; but in 1486, a certain officer named Bahadur Gelauce, got the command of the town by intrigue and violence. In 1495 that usurper having been slain in a battle against Mahmood, Emperor of the Deccan, the government was given to one Mullek-Eia-al-Moolk, whose son and successor, bearing the same name, acknowledge himself, in 1497, the vassal of Adilshaw or Idalkhan, as the Portuguese call him, but who had since 1489, declared himself King or Sultan of Bijapoor, though he still nominally acknowledged the supremacy of the Deccanese Monarch. Such was the state of Goa, when Vasco de Gama landed at Calicut, with the first Portuguese fleet that had yet appeared in India. When the Admiral was about to return to Portugal, a Polonian Jew, giving himself for an Italian, and Prime Minister to Zabajo, King of Goa, came to offer him the alliance of his master; but he was found out afterwards to be a spy and an imposter, and was taken to Portugal where he embraced the Christian religion, and having had Gama himself for his godfather, took the name of Gasper de Gama. The story of this Jew is certain, and this circumstance related by the Portuguese seems to contradict the account of Ferishta; but besides that the Jew, having been an imposter, might have said what he pleased, and given any name to the pretended King of Goa, it is not impossible that the Portuguese authors have disfigured the name, according to their custom, and that the King in question was either Mullek-Eia-al-Moolk or Adilshaw himself, whom they call afterwards actually King of Goa, as they also call him King of Balagate: even as they describe the Sultan of Ahmednugur King of Chowl, and that of Guzerat King of Cambay. The ruth is, that Adilshaw or Idalkhan, particularly desired the residence of Goa; and State reasons alone prevented him from transporting the seat of his Government thither from Bijapore. This predilection, the affluence of the Mahometans, and the liberty of commerce, greatly augmented the prosperity of Goa, and determined the great Alfonso de Albuquerque, second Portuguese Governor of India, to undertake the conquest of that important place, and make it the metropolis and emporium of his countrymen in the East. Accordingly, on the 7th of February of the year 1510, he entered the harbour with a fleet, which had sailed from Cochin, aided by the vessels of the Rajah of Onor the enemy of the Moors, surprised the garrison and made himself master of the town. Shortly after, having gone to visit the other settlements, Adilshaw hastened from Bijapoor and crossing the canal laid siege to the town. The Portuguese garrison, which little expected him, hastily betook themselves to their vessels and put to sea, abandoning the place to the Mahometants; but soon after Albuquerque returned anon with his fleet, and the garrison left by Adilshaw, who had gone back to Bijapoor, surrendered. Since that time Goa ever remained subject to the Portuguese; and is to this day the metropolis of all their Eastern dominions. As it was on the 25th of November, 1510, when it became subjected for the second time to the Portuguese sway, and as that day is dedicated in the Roman Calendar to the memory of the celebrated Virgin and Martyr of Alexandria, St. Catherine, she was chosen for the patroness of the city; a church or rather a chapel was immediately raised in her honour, which still exists, and in which every year her festival, and the anniversary of the victory of the Portuguese, are celebrated with the greatest solemnity by the Franciscan friars, who have the care of the place, in the presence of all the secular and regular clergy and of the Viceroy or Governor, who puts on during the Mass the red habit of the brotherhood of the Saint, of which he is a member, as well as all the magistrates of the city. Soon after this second conquest of Goa, Albuquerque took care not only to repair and augment the fortifications of the town but to strengthen the weak parts of the shore of the island, by which the enemy might cross over and get into it from the continent. This last step, which was however not perfectly carried into effect until sixty years after, was nevertheless most necessary of the two; as the rapid increase of population in the town, necessitating the erection of new houses on all sides, soon rendered the walls useless. Albuquerque spared indeed no pain to render the city the most flourishing in the East. He greatly embellished it by the erection of palaces and churches; he established laws and tribunals, encouraged commerce, caused a mint to be erected, and money to be coined in the name of Emmanuel, King of Portugal; he greatly favoured the marriages between the European settlers and the natives. From this period to the year 1571, Goa continued to prosper, and at last attained the meridian of its glory. It had been raised to the dignity of a Bishopric in 1534, and to that of Archbishopric and Primary of the East Indies in 1557, as we shall notice hereafter. The Viceroy Antonio de Noronha, who had the administration of Portuguese India from 1567 to 1571, built that great wall which is still on the N. E. side of the town, and goes along all the eastern coast of the island, having three gates, that of Dowji, that of the Dry passage, so-called on account of the shallowness of the channel in that place, and that of St. Yago. From this gate, the wall has been continued since in a western direction, reaching the summit of the hill or mountain which is on the south side of the Augustinian convent, where a kind of battery was erected, the remains of which still exist. The old wall of the city having tumbled down, Goa never had any other fortification, besides those towards the harbour, but the above mentioned exterior ramparts, which include, besides the space occupied by the city and its eastern and southern suburbs, when it was most extensive, the country parishes and villages of St. Joseph or upper Dowji, St. Blasius, St Yago, Carambolim, St. Simon, Asocim and Corlim, which were never considered as part of the town.

In 1570, Goa was afflicted with a contagious disease, which swept away a considerable number of the inhabitants ; and the following year, it was besieged by Ali I., 5th King of Bijapoor, whom the Portuguese call Idal Khan, King of Balagate, as they do his predecessors. The enemy having retired, it appears that Goa soon retrieved its losses, and that the population continued to augment or at least remained stationary. In 1582, the same year that Philip II., King of Spain, got himself acknowledged as King of Portugal, Fre Vincent de Fonçeca, of the Order of St. Dominic, whom that Prince named to the Archbishopric of Goa, arrived thither from Europe with a Dutch-man, named John Hugh Linschoten, native of Harlem in Holland, in quality of one of his domestics or pages, an office till now, but much more at that period, held in great consideration. This man, who does not seem to have embraced the information that many of his countrymen had done, passed first into Spain, to which all the Netherlands then submitted, and afterwards into Portugal, upon the annexion of that kingdom to the Spanish monarchy ; and took occasion of the friendship which the new Archbishop bore him, to go down to India, being solely incited by the desire of improving his knowledge by travelling. Upon his return to his native country, after years spent in the East, but chiefly in Goa, he published an account of his adventures, and of the countries which he visited, in the old gothic French language as spoken in his time in most parts of Europe. He expatiates a great deal on Goa, and even gives a figurative plan of the city and of the whole island, with a description of all the buildings which then existed. Although the plan is not drawn on a proper scale, it suffices nevertheless to give us an exact idea of the extent of the city at that early period, that is only 72 years after its conquests by the Portuguese. To the East the compact streets and the buildings extended as far as Lower Dowji or St. Lucia, where it communicated by a cause way, with a continued series of buildings on the land side to the parish of Upper Dowji, which might be then considered as a suburb, in which were a palace belonging to the senate, still standing near the passage or ferry to the island of Naroa, and the convent of the Mother of God, of the Order of St. Francis, which is now the provincial house of the reformed Franciscans or recollects. From St. Lucia the city extended southerly as far as the hospital of St. Lazarus, including the large inclosure of the Dominican convent, and the mountain on which was built several years ago, the chapel and hermitage still existing of *Nossa Senhora de Monte.* The great and broad street of St. Paul communicated, with very few interruptions, with the buildings near the village and the passage of St. Yago. The southern limits were formed by the large pond or *Lagoa*, behind the parochial church of the Holy Trinity, (the stagnant waters whereof infected by the carcase of a dead elephant, are thought to have occasioned the pestilence which we spoke of a little before), and afterwards by the valley that separates the mountain, on which the new convent of the congregation of St. Philip Neri now stands, from that of *Nossa Senhora de Luz*, which last with its parochial church was comprehended within the city. To the S. W. the buildings extended almost to old Goa, and from that point towards the north, reached the old western walls to the gate that was taken down at the end of the street of Ormutz, and near the foot of the mountain of the Rosary; where, after a short causeway, lined with houses on the southern side, began the suburb of St. Peter or Pannely, which at the other end communicated as it does still, with the village of Ribandar, by an almost continued series of buildings; but the fine causeway, which now extends to Pangi, was formed near a century afterwards by the Jesuits.

The city, thus bounded, exclusive of St. Peter and the other suburbs abovementioned, was about a mile and a half in length, from east to west, and nearly as much in breadth, and about six miles in circumference. At that time it was divided into six parishes, besides those of the suburbs and the extra parochial church in the King's arsenal. At the arrival of the Governor Martin Alfonso de Sousa in 1542, all Goa was comprehended in the parish of the Cathedral ; but during his administration, three new parishes were erected, and separated from it. Two were added since that period to that in which Linchosten wrote. The public buildings were then, the Cathedral, the adjoining Archiepiscopal palace, the palace of the Governor, the Custom-house, and the King's arsenal, on the very same spots where they are now seen, whether entire or in ruins. Between the Governor's palace and the convent of St. Dominic, beyond a small inlet for boats, were the great Bazar and the Bangasal or Warehouse, on the space since occupied by the convent of St. Cajetan and its dependencies. The Senate chamber or *camara*, wherein the courts of justice were held, and the palace of the inquisition, were then opposite one another on the two sides of the Cathedral square as they are still. The King's Hospital was then contiguous to the arsenal; that of the poor, in the street leading to Trinity Church, where the remains are still extant. The principal shops and the Exchange or *Leilão* were in the place where we now see the present wretched bazar. There were then but five male convents, of which two belonged to the Jesuits, within the city, besides that of the Mother of God in Dowji, which we have mentioned, and not a single Nunnery. "So difficult is it," says Linchosten, "for the Goa females to devote themselves to the laws of celibacy!" The buildings of Misericordia indeed are marked on his plan, and existed a long time before, but they were then merely appropriated to a religious confraternity and association of the principal citizens; and the three houses of retreat for men, widows and virgins, were only erected at the expense of the Institution, under Archbishop Alexo de Menezes who filled this metropolitan See from 1595 to 1616. Under that celebrated Archbishop, whose memory is held in such veneration in India and in Portugal, but who is represented in such black colours by the English Authors, it was deemed necessary to erect a new parish within the town, which proves that notwithstanding the neglect which the Portuguese settlements in India experienced from the Court of Madrid, and notwithstanding the trade which the Dutch and English began to carry on in this part of the world, to the detriment of the Portuguese, the population of Goa, far from diminishing, continued to augment. It is rather difficult to form a just estimate of the total population of Goa at the beginning of the seventeenth century; but from what I have heard concerning the number of communicants, in the different parishes as they are transmitted by the records, the number must have been about 150,000 professing the Christian religion. The strangers, Banians, and other Hindoos, and Mahometans, may have amounted to about 50,000 more, giving a total of 200,000 for the city; exclusive of the suburbs, concerning which it is impossible to form any probable conjecture. This number might appear small in proportion to the extent of the place we are speaking of, but it must be considered that the public buildings, chiefly the King's Arsenal and the convents, occupied large spaces of ground. Linchosten informs us that the principal houses were large, but not high, and surrounded with spacious gardens for the benefit of the air. Besides, the Mahometans and Hindoos were allowed to sojourn in Goa, but to exercise no public act of their religion; they were however not so many in number as in the other great trading towns of India, and only such as were attracted by commerce and the desire of lucre.

In 1603, the Dutch blockaded Goa with their fleet, but were soon after obliged to withdraw: however, as they began now to command the trade of the East, they considerably annoyed and diminished that of the Portuguese; and it is from this period and not before that Goa began to decline. It does not seem nevertheless that this diminution was very apparent, chiefly among the population of the city, till about forty years after. The harbour was again blockaded by the Dutch in 1643, who about the same time took Ceylon, Malacca, and the Moluccas from the Portuguese, whom they excluded likewise by their intrigues and influence from the trade of Japan. Poverty now began to increase so rapidly in Goa, that Tavernier, who visited it in 1642 and in 1648, tells us that many of the inhabitants, who at the time of his first voyage enjoyed incomes of 2,000 crowns, were reduced to beg alms secretly, when he arrived the second time. He intimates likewise that the city was not then very populous, which he attributes to the excessive heat of the climate. Dellon, who resided in this city thirty years later, represents it indeed as considerably decayed, but says it was still a large and very important city.

This is however not the case with the Jesuit Antonio de Sousa, who published his work entitled Oriente Conquistado in the beginning of the eighteenth century; he affirms that Goa, from a large and opulent metropolis, was then no more than the chief town of a most miserable territory. The unhealthiness of the city, in which the presence of the few rich inhabitants that remained was no longer necessary in consequence of the decline of business, caused them to remove to the country on their lands, to enjoy the revenues thereof and breathe a more salubrious air. By this time all the settlements of the Coast of Malabar had been taken by the Dutch; Sevaji, the founder of the Maharatta empire, had threatened Goa by land in 1674, and his successors continued to annoy the Portuguese. The fortress of Ponda, on the mainland, was then the chief object of their attacks, and though taken and retaken, proved at that period the true bulwark of Goa.

The consternation of the Goanese augmented in 1737 and 1739, under the Viceroy Pedro de Mascarenhas, when the fort of Tanna, with the whole island of Salsette, and the important city of Basseen or Bacaim, with its territory, were wrested from the Portuguese by the Mahrattas, who, soon after, made an irruption into the peninsula of Bardes, only a few miles from Goa. The increase of the British power, and the close alliance which united the courts of London and Lisbon, the protection which the French gave to the Nizam of the Deccan, and to the Nabob of the Carnatic, checked the progress of the Mahrattas, and prevented further encroachments. Peace was concluded between the Viceroy of Goa and the Peshwa, and a Resident was sent to Poona. In 1759, a solemn *Te Deum* was sung in the Cathedral on this occasion. From that year, although the decline and depopulation of the city continued, the neighbouring provinces dependant on it began on the contrary to wear a new aspect; and their prosperity was considerably augmented by the security which the inhabitants enjoyed. The town of Margaon, in the peninsula of Salsette, and that of Mapuça, in that of Bardes, began rapidly to increase; and the village of Pangi obtained a great lustre and importance from the Viceroy fixing his habitual residence in it. The old Palace or *Casa de Polvora*, in St. Peter or Pannely, was transformed into a Royal Hospital, that of the city having been pulled down. The Governors or Viceroys continued however to occupy the old palace of the city which was still in good repair, and has been entirely abandoned only since about twenty years. The suppression of the Jesuits was a new misfortune to the city of Goa and the colony at large, by the desertion of their five beautiful houses, two of which have fallen into ruins. and still more by the deterioration which was experienced in the education of youth, chiefly of the clergy, who were but very imperfectly replaced by some Italian Lazarists, to whom their chief house of *Bom-Jesus* was entrusted for some time, and a great deal more by the priests of St. Philip de Neri, all natives of the Brahminical caste, who are now the only masters in the two seminaries of Chorão and Rachol.

The oldest men I have consulted have all assured me, that they do not remember to have seen the town of Goa in a state much superior to that in which we now see it. Two of the parish churches are abandoned and in ruins; the others, except the cathedral, are fast decaying, being only opened on Sundays and Festival days, and are entirely destitute of repairs, in consequence of the small number of their parishioners, not amounting altogether to 100, which, with 120 in the parish of the cathedral, makes the whole number, exclusive of the clergy, monks, nuns and their servants, the inmates of the *Casas de Misericordia*, and the people employed in the arsenal, to be only 220 or 250, at most; but the population of the suburb of St. Peter or Pannely has increased to about 1500, and so of Ribandar, and still more Pangi, as we will say in another Section.

S. II.—*Chronological Table of the Viceroys and Governors of Goa, and Portuguese India—from the conquest to the present time—with the most memorable events in each administration.*

Don Francisco de Almeida, first Viceroy of India, in 1505, resided commonly on the island of Anjediva or at Cochin.

1509.—Alfonso de Albuquerque, the greatest hero of Portuguese Asia, succeeded Almeida this year in the month of November, with only the title of Governor, after running in imminent danger at the court of the Zamorin, or Sovereign of Calicut, whence he extricated himself by his invincible courage and the love of his soldiers. He took Goa from the Mahometans on the 17th of February, 1510; but it having been retaken shortly after by Adilshaw or Idul Khan, during his absence, he got possession of it a second time on the 25th November the same year. He took Malacca the year following, and in 1515 sailed for Ormutz, in the Persian Gulf; but hearing that he had incurred the displeasure of his Sovereign, and had been superseded in the Government of India, he returned to Goa and died as he entered the harbour. He was truly a great man in every respect. When justice was at last rendered to his memory in Portugal, his remains were transported from Goa to Lisbon, not without much opposition or regret on the part of the inhabitants of the first of those cities.

1515.—Lopez Soarez de Albargaria, Governor, who, after three years, returned to Portugal.

1518.—Diego Lopez de Siqueira, Governor, who remained for the same space of time, and returned also to Portugal.

1521.—Duarte de Menezes I, Governor, id.........id.

1524.—Vasco de Gama, Count of Almirante, the discoverer of the way to India by the Cape of Good Hope, and the first Portuguese Admiral in the Indian Seas, was sent to Goa in this year, with the title of Viceroy of India, which none had yet been dignified with since Almeida; but he died four months after at Cochin.

1525.—Henri de Menezes succeeded Gama as acting Governor but would not enter into office or allow any rejoicings on that occasion, until he had performed the last duties to his illustrious predecessor; saying, that it was much more becoming to bewail the loss of that great man, than to rejoice at his assuming the administration. He died in Cannanore in February the following year.

1526.—Lopo Vas de Sampayo, Governor. During his administration, Ridor in the Moluccas, Mangalore on the Malabar Coast, and the island of Maim or Bombay, were taken possession of by the Portuguese. After three years he returned to Portugal.

1529.—Nunho de Cunha succeeded this year as Governor. He took the cities of Bassoen or Bacaim and of Daman from Bahadur Shah, King of Guzerat and afterwards the stronghold and island of Diu, on the coast of the Peninsula of the same kingdom, now called Kattywar, after a long and memorable siege. It was during this siege, that a soldier near the General having had his head struck off by a cannon ball, Nunho exclaimed coolly to the by-standers who were filled with terror and bewailing their danger: "*Humiliate capita vestra Deo.*" Humble your heads before God. Thus making use of the words of Scripture, which are employed in a well-known part of the Roman Liturgy. By the terror which his name inspired, his successor after the capitulation, concluded an advantageous and glorious peace with Bahadur Shah, whom the Portuguese authors call King of Cambay, which was his chief sea-port. He made a formal cession of Bombay, Chawl, Basseen, Daman and Diu. Nunho de Cunha having been recalled after nine years' administration, died on his way home.

1538.—Gracias de Noronha, 3rd Viceroy of India, arrived this year, and died nineteen months after in Goa. He was buried in the Cathedral.

1539.—Stephen de Gama, son of the hero of that name, succeeded as acting Governor. He undertook a celebrated expedition into the Red Sea; went as far as Mount Sinai, in Arabia to the shrine of St. Catherine, patroness of Goa, where he raised himself to the honour of knighthood, which he afterwards bestowed himself on all his companions, among whom were Alvarez de Castro, son of the future celebrated Viceroy of that name, and Lewis de Almeida who afterwards distinguished himself so gloriously in Germany, under the Emperor Charles V., that he would then have obtained knighthood from that prince, if he had not already possessed that dignity. On this occasion, the Emperor said that he esteemed more the honour he had had of being knighted by the son of Gama, on Mount Sinai, than the victory he had just gained; as for Castro, father of Alvarez, he set such a great value on the honour bestowed on his son, that to perpetuate the memory of it, he put the wheel of St. Catherine in his family arms.

1542.—Alfonso Martin de Souza, Governor, arrived this year in India, having the celebrated Francis Xaverious or Xavier with him. Japan was discovered. The first great spiritual labours and achievements of Francis Xavier signalized this administration; and Goa increased considerably. After three years, Souza returned to Portugal.

1545.—John de Castro, called by some authors, the last Portuguese hero in the East, equalled his most illustrious predecessors, by his virtues and the glory he acquired both as a warrior and a statesman. He succeeded Souza, only with the title of Governor. He defeated Ibrahim, King of Bijapoor, and secured to the crown of Portugal the two peninsulas of Salsette and Bardes, which encompass the island of Goa. He afterwards sent his son Ferdinand to succour John de Mascarenhas, Governor of Diu, who was besieged in the citadel by Mahomet, King of Guzerat, successor of Bahadur, assisted by a Turkish fleet and the troops of the King of Bijapoor, commanded by Allad Khan, his prime minister. Ferdinand having been killed, Castro did not hesitate to send his second son Alvarez, who had been knighted at Mount Sinai; he afterwards went himself with a fleet, penetrated into the citadel, from which he went out to give battle to the enemies, and gained over them a most complete and glorious victory. Being afterwards in want of money to continue the war, which was not terminated, he sent to Goa, to borrow the sum he wanted, with one of his whiskers as security. That pledge was received with due honour, and more than the sum required was procured. The ladies of Goa and Chawl even sent him all their jewels, which Castro refused courteously after praising them for their patriotism. Castro having put all the enemies to flight on every side, and having concluded peace, celebrated a triumph on his re-entering Goa, after the manner of the ancients, pulling down a part of the walls to raise the triumphal arch. Sometime after, he fell into a lingering disease, which made him soon disgusted of all worldly things, and made him turn his thoughts entirely to the solid goods of eternity. Xavier having about this time returned from the Moluccas, he chose him as the director of his conscience; and having gone back to Goa, in order to correct what his former triumph had, contrary to Christian humility, induced him to do, he caused a second one to be celebrated, attributing the whole glory to the Almighty, and to the intercession of the Apostle St. Thomas and of St. Martin whose images he ordered to be set up in the place of his own. Soon after, being confined to his bed, despatches arrived from Portugal, by which he was dignified with the title of Viceroy, and was continued in his office for three years longer. The people made public rejoicings, and a great display of fireworks on that occasion. Castro, hearing their shouts and seeing the illumination from his windows, said to Xavier, who was seated at his bedside : "*How deceitful is this world which promises three years' honours to a man who has but a few moments to live.* He expired some days after, in the same Christian sentiments, in the arms of Francis Xavier, who assisted him to his last breath: a remarkable circumstance, that the greatest Christian hero of the East, should have died attended by the most illustrious Apostle of that part of the world in modern times. Castro died so poor that the city was obliged to defray the expenses of his funeral.

1548.—Gracias de Sa succeeded as acting Governor; under him the King of Tanor came to Goa, and embraced the Christian religion. After one year, Gracias de Sa died, and was buried in the church of *Nossa Senhora de Rosario.*

1549.—George Cabral, acting Governor. He returned to Portugal after about two years' administration.

1551.—Alfonso de Noronha, Viceroy. In his time, Francis Xavier died in the island of Sancian, near Canton in China, and his body was translated first to Malacca, and thence to Goa. Noronha died after four years of his administration.

1554.—Peter de Mascarenhas, Viceroy.

1555.—Francis de Barreto, acting Governor. He returned to Portugal after about four years.

1558.—Constantine de Braganza, Viceroy. He was of the royal blood: his name has remained dear to the Portuguese of India. He was the constant friend and protector of the celebrated Lewis Camoens, author of the *Lusiade.* He was firm, wise, mild, polite and benevolent; but he has nevertheless incurred the hatred of foreign historians, because the too famous tribunal of the Inquisition was established in Goa during his administration, although he had no hand in that business, which took place long before in Portugal; we shall however speak more on that subject in the next paragraph. Constantine is also blamed and ridiculed, for having refused to give to the King of Pegue a tooth, (which some affirm to have been that of a monkey), but which had been revered as that of

Buddha in a temple of Jaffnapatam in Ceylon, although that prince offered for it 300,000 cruzados; in this business Constantine acted as a conscientious and religious man; he consulted the Archbishop and Clergy on this occasion, as he was afraid on the one hand of participating in an act of idolatry and superstition, and on the other of defrauding the King, his master, of a considerable treasure; and when it was made clear to him that, according to conscience and natural reason, it was unlawful to participate in an act of idolatry for any reason whatsoever, much less for a sum of money, which would be adding to the former guilt, that of avarice, he immediately consented that the infamous relic should be thrown into the sea. If he had taken the money, he would certainly have been represented by the prejudiced authors, as a covetous man without law or conscience; but as he acted otherwise they call him a fool. It is very difficult or rather impossible to please those who are bent on blaming their fellow-creatures. After three years, this nobleman returned to Portugal.

1561.—Francis Coutinho, Count of Redondo, Viceroy. After two years, he died in Goa.

1563.—John de Mendose, acting Governor.

1564.—Antonio de Noronha I., Viceroy. He was almost equally beloved with Constantine Braganza. He built that long wall along the eastern shore of the island of Goa, to defend it from any aggression from the continent. He died in 1568, on his passage back to Portugal.

1568.—Lewis de Ataida, Viceroy. Under him Goa was afflicted with a pestilence as we have said in the preceding paragraph; it was thought to have been caused by the carcase of an elephant, stuck fast in the *Lagoa* or pond, adjoining Trinity church. It was also during the first part of Ataida's administration, that Goa was besieged by Ali Adilshaw or Idalkhan, king of Bijapoor.

1571.—Antonio de Noronha II., son of the former Viceroy of that name. He governed two years, and returned to Europe.

1573.—Antonio Monis Barreto, Governor during three years, after which he was recalled.

1576.—Diego de Menezes, Governor during two years.

1578.—Lewis d'Ataide, Viceroy for the second time; he died in Goa.

1580.—Ferdinand Telles, acting Governor for seven months.

1581.—Francis de Mascarenhas, Viceroy, sent by Philip II., of Spain, who took possession in that year of the throne of Portugal. After three years he returned to Europe.

1584.—Duarte de Menezes II., descended from the first Governor of that name, arrived as Viceroy of India, and after more than three years died in Goa.

1588.—Emanuel de Sousa Coutinho, acting Governor, was confirmed, and continued three years in office.

1590.—Matthias de Albuquerque, Viceroy. He governed for more than six years.

1597.—Francis de Gama, Count of Vidigneira, Admiral of India, great grandson of Vasco, came to India as a Viceroy at the age of 31, and returned to Portugal after three years' administration.

1600.—Ayres de Saldanha, Viceroy, governed four years. During his administration the Dutch blockaded Goa for the first time.

1604.—Martin Alfonso de Castro, son of the hero of the same name. He delivered Malacca, which was besieged by the fleet of the King of Java; and died in that city in 1647.

1607.—Fré Alexo de Menezes, Archbishop of Goa, administered as acting Governor in the absence, and after the death of his predecessor; more shall be said of him hereafter.

1609.—Andrew Furtado de Mendoza, acting Governor, confirmed afterwards for three years.

1612.—Jerom de Azavedo, Viceroy for four years.

1617.—John Coutinho, Count of Redondo, son of the Viceroy of that name, came to India in the same quality, and died about two years after at Goa.

1619.—Ferdinand de Albuquerque, who was before Governor of Colombo, in Ceylon, and had been fifty-one years in India, succeeded as acting Governor of all India. He remained more than three years in office.

1622.—Francis de Gama, Count of Vidigneira, Admiral of India, Viceroy for the second time, governed during five years.

1627.—Fr. Lewis de Brito, of the order of St. Augustine, Bishop of Meliapor and Bishop-elect of Cochin, who had been twice Governor of the Settlements of the Coromandel Coast, succeeded as acting Governor of India and died in Goa.

1629.—Miguel de Noronha, Viceroy, administered during six years, and caused several useful works to be executed; amongst others, the great bridge of Pangi, assisted by the influence of the Jesuits.

1635.—Peter de Silva, Viceroy, died on the 24th of June in 1639 in Goa, and was buried in the church of St. Dominic.

1639.—Antonio Tellis, acting Governor.

1640.—John de Silva Tello de Menezes, Viceroy. Under him Goa was severally attacked by the Dutch. The Duke of Braganza was proclaimed King in this year under the name of John IV. and Portugal became again an independent State. After five years John de Silva returned to Europe.

1645.—Philip de Mascarenhas succeeded as Viceroy at the end of this year, and governed until 1651, when he died on his way home. It was under this Viceroy that the decline of Goa became so sensible, as Tavernier informs us who visited it during this administration.

1651.—Antonio de Souza Coutinho, Fre Francis de Martyres, Archbishop of Goa, and Francis de Mello de Castro governed by *interim*, having learned the death of Count John de Silva Tello de Menezes, Viceroy, which had taken place on his passage to India; so that both the old and new Viceroy died at sea.

1652.—Vasco de Mascarenhas, Viceroy, was forced to embark for Europe, during a sedition of the people.

1655.—Rodrigo de Silveira, Count of Sargedas, Viceroy, died in 1656, and was buried at the Dominicans.

1656.—Emanuel Mascarenhas, Francis de Mello de Castro, and Antonio de Sousa Coutinho, governed jointly; but the first dying the same year, the two others continued in office till 1661.

1661.—Lewis de Mendoça Furtado Albuquerque, Governor during one year.

1662.—Peter de Lancaster. He governed for a short time.

1662.—Antonio de Mello, Viceroy. In his time, Cochin and the settlements of the Coast of Malabar, were taken by the Dutch.

1666.—John Nunho de Cunha, Count of St. Vincent, Viceroy, died two years after, and was buried in the church of *Bom-Jesus*, which is that of the professed house of Jesuits.

1668.—Antonio de Mello de Castro, son of the last Viceroy but one before him, became acting Governor.

1671.—Lewis de Mendoça Furtado Albuquerque, Count of Lauzadio, Viceroy. He governed during nearly seven years.

1677.—Peter de Almeida, Viceroy, died in Mosambique in 1679.

1678.—Fre Antonio Brandão, Archbishop of Goa, and Antonio Paes de Saude, administered jointly during the late Viceroy's absence; but the Archbishop dying in July the same year, the latter was sole acting Governor for more than four years.

1682.—Francis de Taura, Count of Alvordo, Viceroy. He carried on a successful war with Sambaji, the Mahratta; fortified the island of Angediva, administered during four years with zeal and activity, and returned to Portugal.

1686.—Rodrigo de Costa, acting Governor, died three years after, and was buried in the church of *Bom-Jesus.*

1690.—Miguel de Almeida, acting Governor, died the following year and was buried in the church of the college of St. Thomas Aquinas belonging to the Dominicans.

1691.—Ferdinand Martin Mascarenhas and Lewis Gonzalves Costa administered jointly; but the latter dying in June 1622, Fr. Augustine de Annunciação, the new Archbishop, who arrived in Goa, was associated to the government in September following.

1693.—Pedro Antonio de Noronha, Count of Villaverde, Viceroy; he returned to Europe after the arrival of his successor.

1698.—Antonio Lewis Gonzalves de Camara Coutinho, Viceroy. He administered during three years, and died at Bahia, in Brasils, on his way home.

1701.—Fré Augustine de Annunciação, Archbishop of Goa, and Vasco Lewis Coutinho, administered jointly as acting Governors.

1702.—Caetano de Mello de Castro, Viceroy, governed Portuguese India for fi · years, with courage and activity.

1707.—Rodrigo da Costa, Viceroy, governed also for five years.

1712.—Vasco Ferdinand Cesar de Menezes, Viceroy, for the same period of time.

1717.—Sebastião de Andrade Passanha, Archbishop of Goa, acting Governor from January till October.

1717.—Lewis de Menezes, Count of Ereceira, Viceroy. He sent an embassy to the King of Persia, and afterwards a fleet to succour that Prince against the Arabs. After three years, he returned to Portugal.

1720.—Francis Joseph de Sampayo-e-Castro, Viceroy. After three years, he died in Goa, and was buried in the professed house of the Jesuits.

1723.—Christopher de Mello, acting Governor, from July to September.

1723.—Ignatio de Santa Theresa, Archbishop of Goa, Christopher de Mello, and Christopher Lewis de Andrade, administered jointly, (by virtue of letters received to that effect from the Court of Portugal), until October, 1725.

1725.—John de Saldanha de Gama, Viceroy for upwards of six years, during which Goa was in perpetual fear and consternation, occasioned by the neighbouring States and the progress of the Mahratta armies. He at last obtained leave to return to Portugal.

1732.—Ignatio de Santa Theresa, Archbishop of Goa, Christopher de Mello, and Thomas Gomes Moreira, governed jointly till November the same year.

1732.—Peter de Mascarenhas, Count of Sandomit, Viceroy. He governed near nine years. In his time, Tanna and the whole island of Salsette, near Bombay, the important city of Basseen or Bacaim, with its dependencies, Zarapour, the island of Caranja, in fine, all that composed the province called *del·Norte*, except Daman and Diu, were taken by the Mahrattas, who had also invaded the peninsulas of Salsette and Bardes, and threatened Goa itself. To complete the calamities of the Portuguese in the East, their fleet was destroyed by the Angria pirate. The unfortunate Viceroy returned to Portugal in 1742, after the arrival of his successor with powerful forces.

1741.—Lewis de Menezes, Marquis of Lourical, Viceroy, having arrived in Goa with 12,000 men from the Brasils, delivered the provinces of Bardes and Salsette, and ordered the famous fort of Ponda, on the mainland, to be besieged. The very day that it was taken by the Portuguese, the 12th of June 1742, the Viceroy died in the Palace *de Polvora* in the suburb of St. Peter or Pannely, and his body was transported with great pomp to the professed house of the Jesuits, where it was interred at the foot of the altar of St. Francis Xavier.

1742.—Francis de Vasconcellos, Bishop of Cochin, Laurance de Noronha, and Lewis Cætano de Almeida, were found named jointly at the death of the late Viceroy. The first however being in his diocese, and the second in Mosambique, where he was Governor, the third alone assumed the administration, which he filled till December. The Bishop arrived in Goa by this time, but died in March following in the Palace *de Polvora*, and was buried in the church of *Bom-Jesus;* in consequence of which, Almeida again governed alone till the arrival of his colleague from Mosambique in May following, after which they governed jointly for more than a year.

1743.—Pedro Miguel de Almeida-e-Portugal, Count of Assumar, and Marquis of Castellonovo, Viceroy. He carried on a successful war with the Mahrattas, from whom he took the fortreses of Bicholim and Sanquelim, on the mainland, to the east of Bardes, with the surrounding territories which still belong to Portugal; after the arrival of his successor he returned to Europe.

1750.—Francis de Tavra, Marquis of Tavra and Count of St. John, Viceroy. He carried on a successful war, by sea and land, against the Mahrattas, and after four years returned home.

1754.—Lewis de Mascarenhas, Count of Alva, Viceroy. He continued the war with the Mahrattas, but having besieged Ponda, which had been retaken by the enemy, he was killed in the attack, on the 22nd of June 1756; his body was transported to Goa, and interred at the Jesuits.

1756.—Antonio Taveira de Neiva-e-Boum, Archbishop of Goa, John Mesquita, Mattos Texeira, and Philip Valadares Souto Mayor, administered during the vacancy.

1758.—Emanuel de Saldanha de Albuquerque, Count of Ega, Viceroy. He continued the war, and concluded an advantageous peace with the Mahratta, for which a solemn *Te Deum* was sung in Goa, on the 25th of July 1759. On the 1st of December, the same year, he transferred his habitual residence, from the palace *de Polvora* in Pannely to that of Pangi or Pangim, where, his successors continue to reside to this day. The Royal Hospital of Goa, near the Arsenal, having been pulled down, the old palace of *Polvora* was appropriated to receive the infirm soldiers and sailors, and still continues to be the Royal Hospital. The palace of Goa continued to be inhabited by the Viceroy on certain solemn occasions throughout the year. Ponda and all the new provinces of the mainland, were to be given up to the Mahrattas; but in consequence of the new wars, which that people were involved in, by the contentions between the English and French, and the Nabob of the Carnatic, the Portuguese remained in possession of them, though they had to maintain them by force against the different contending powers. The Count of Ega governed till the end of 1765; when, upon the news of the death of his successor, the Count of Lousaa, on his passage to India, he ordered the sealed letters of the Court to be opened, and having resigned the administration to the Archbishop and his colleagues, returned to Europe.

1765.—Antonio Taveira de Neiva-e-Boum, Archbishop of Goa, John Baptist var Pereira, and John Joseph de Mello, administered the affairs jointly during three years.

1768.—John Joseph de Mello, one of the three mentioned above, was named titular Governor by the Court of Lisbon, and was solely invested with the whole administration by his two former colleagues. He died six years after, and was buried in the convent of Nossa Senhora de Pilar, of the order of the Recollect Franciscans, out of the city.

1774.—Philip de Valadares, acting Governor, from March to September.

1774.—Joseph Pedro de Camara, Governor and Captain-General of India, for five years. The new title of Captain-General had been substituted for that of Viceroy by the Marquis of Pombal, prime minister of Joseph, King of Portugal, whose reputation is so well known.

1779.—Frederic William de Sousa, Governor and Captain-General. He once more united to the crown of Portugal, the provinces of Bicholim and Sanquelim, on the mainland in 1782. After seven years' administration he returned to Portugal.

1786.—Francis de Cunha de Menezes, Governor and Captain-General; he was forced to give up the province of Pernem, on the mainland, to Tippoo Saib, Sultan of Mysore. After eight years, he went back to Europe.

1794.—Francis Antony de Veiga Cabral, Governor and Captain-General; he remained thirteen years in office, during which, the embarrassment of affairs in Europe, caused Goa and the settlements of India, to be much neglected by Portugal, but they, nevertheless improved on the fall of Tippoo, by the restoration of the province of Pernem. In 1801, an English auxiliary force took possession of the forts of Aguada in Bardes and of Cabo on the island of Goa, commanding the entrance of the river, which they retained until the general peace, in 1815.

1807.—Bernard Joseph Lourena, Count of Sargedas, arrived with the double title of Viceroy and Captain-General of Portuguese India, and administered during nine years. In 1812, at the persuasion of the British Government, the Court of Portugal, then residing in the Brasils, abolished the Inquisition; and the palace of that Institution in Goa was shut up.

1816.—Diego de Sousa, Count of Rio Pardo, Viceroy, and Captain-General. He was invested with the administration, according to custom, in the church af *Bom-Jesus*, on the 29th of November.

1821.—In consequence of the political changes in Portugal, a revolution took place in Goa. The Viceroy, Count of Rio Pardo, was arrested, and confined in the fort of Cabo; a council of four members, elected by the inhabitants, was appointed to govern the Colony, on the principle of the *Cortes* then sitting at Lisbon.

1822.—Emanuel de Camara arrived in December this year, as Governor, from Portugal; but was obliged to associate himself with four councillors as his colleagues in the administration.

1822.—Captain Lewis Pratis de Albuquerque, Editor of the *Goa Gazette*, was murdered by conjuration. The Archbishop retired to Sinkeri, in Carwar, under the protection of the British Government; and the former Viceroy, Count de Rio Pardo, having been set at liberty, retired to Bombay.

1824.—King John VI., having recovered his power and dissolved the *Cortes*, sent orders to Dom Manuel de Camara, to govern India after the ancient forms, and to assume the title of Viceroy. Public tranquility was now restored, and the Archbishop returned to Goa.

1826.—Upon the death of the Viceroy, in November this year, Frè Emanuel a Sto. Galdino, Archbishop of Goa, and two others, assumed the administration of public affairs, according to the ancient custom.

1827.—Don Emanuel de Castro é Portugal (a natural branch of the Royal Family) arrived in the month of October with the title of Governor, and Captain General; and was solemnly invested with the administration, by the Archbishop in the church of *Bom-Jesus*.

S. III. *Religious Establishments—Proceedings and Documents concerning the erection of the Episcopal, and afterwards Archiepiscopal, See of Goa—The Chronology of its Bishops, and Archbishops—Its Provincial Councils—The erection of its Religious Buildings, and Religious Institutions.*

1510.—Goa having been taken in the beginning of this year by the great Albuquerque, from Adilshaw or Idal Khan, King of Visapoor or Bijapoor, there was no time to effect any establishments, before that Prince retook the place again, and forced them to return on board their vessels; but on the 25th of November, Albuquerque, having wrested a second time the town and the island from the Mahometans, and that day being consecrated in the church to the memory of St. Catherine, Virgin and Martyr at Alexandria, that virgin was chosen solemnly as the patroness of Goa, and the protectress of the Portuguese in the East; and the first Christian church or chapel was erected to God in her name, towards the centre of the city, and not far from the landing place. It subsists still as a chapel, though it must have been repaired, and probably rebuilt several times. Every year on the festival of the saint, after the morning service is over in the cathedral, the Franciscans perform a second one, with the greatest solemnity in the chapel, in the presence of the Viceroy, (who wears a red cloak, as a member of the brotherhood or confraternity of the Saint), the clergy of the cathedral, a deputation from all the other churches and convents, the senate, and all the authorities, civil and military.

The Franciscans of the observance, were the first spiritual pastors of the Portuguese in Goa. They, therefore, soon laid the foundation of a convent, which has since been enlarged, and which is the most ancient in Goa. They built adjoining to it a conventual church which is sufficiently large and much admired to this very day, for the style of its architecture, and for its decorations. In consequence of the smallness of the first chapel of St. Catherine, they built also at the public expense, a parochial church, very near likewise to their convent, which became the cathedral, and was afterwards considerably enlarged as we shall see.

The Dominicans came to Goa shortly after its conquest, but they did not form themselves into a community till near half a century after. They built the church of Our Lady of the Rosary on a prominent hill, in the western part of the town. It was afterwards converted into a parochial and collegiate church, and is still in existence. Near this church, is the chapel of St. Anthony of Padua or of Lisbon, as the Portuguese call him, and whom they acknowledge as the patron of their nation. This edifice which was also erected soon after the conquest, and those already mentioned, including the church of Our Lady of Light, (*La Luz*), on a hill towards the south of the town, the chapel of Our Lady of the Mount, in the eastern part, and the hospital of St. Lazarus, are the religious edifices in Goa.

1514.—Bull of Leo X, submitting, as to spirituals, all the conquests of the Portuguese in Africa and Asia, to the Vicar of Thomar, grand master of the Order of Christ, and invested with the episcopal character and consecration.

1515.—Erection, by the same Pope, of the Bishopric of Fonchal, in the island of Madeira; the diocese to comprehend all the Portuguese possessions beyond seas; and the first Bishop of this See, was Don Diego de Pinhero, vicar of Thomar, and grand master of the Order of Christ.

1533.—Madeira or Fonchal is erected into an archiepiscopal or metropolitan See by Clement VII.

1534.—First November, Paul III. successor of Clement VII, erects the Bishopric of Angra, in the island of Tercera, one of the Azores or western islands, that of St. James, of Cape de Verd Islands, that of the island of St. Thomas, near the coast of Guinea, and that of Goa, the diocese of which was to comprehend all the Portuguese Settlements, from the Cape of Good Hope to the extremities of the East. All the Sees were to form the province, and be the Suffragan Bishoprics of Madeira; but the latter See soon became again a simple Bishopric, and together with its four Suffragan Bishoprics, made a part of the ecclesiastical province of Lisbon.

1537.—D. Fr. John of Albuquerque, a Franciscan monk, related to the hero of that name, became first Bishop of Goa; the chapter was founded the very year of his arrival.

1541.—The foundation of the Seminary of the Holy Faith (*Santa Fè*), was laid by the exertions of two secular priests, Michael Vae and James Borba, and by the liberality of the Governor Stephen de Gama, for the instruction of the new converted Indians. Borba became the first superior of this establishment.

1542.—The celebrated St. Francis Xavier arrived in India with the new Governor Martin de Souza. In a few months, he changes entirely the wicked and debauched morals of the Portuguese in Goa, and re-establishes the practice of religion and the frequentation of sacraments. After one year, he goes to the *Connah* of the Paravas or the fishermen of the coast, near Cape Comorin; but during the ten remaining years of his life, which he spent in the East, he made Goa the chief place of his residence, and established therein the chief house of his order in India.

1543.—Borba makes a public cession and abandonment of the church, and seminary of *Santa Fè* to Xavier and his companions; that is, to the members of the order of the Jesuits, who were thus the 2nd order, settled in Goa, in a regular community. The seminary of Santa Fè changed its name into that of St. Paul, from a picture of the conversion of that Apostle, which was placed over the altar in the church; it happened from this, and the celebrity which that college soon acquired, that the Jesuits were known in India, under the name of Fathers of

St. Paul or *Paulistas;* and sometimes likewise, under that of *Apostles*, as they became the chief apostolical preachers in the East.

1545.—This year, which was the last of the administration of the Governor Souza, and the first of that of John de Castro, the city of Goa, which had formed hitherto but one single parish, was divided into four, viz: that of the Cathedral, those of the churches of the Rosary and *Luz*, of which we have already spoken, and which became collegiates, and that of St. Lucia, in the eastern suburbs of the city near the river.

1548.—The foundation of the great Convent and church of the Dominicans, in the western part of the city, was laid. This order was the 3rd, regularly established in Goa. In this year, the Christian religion made great progress in the city and island of Goa, in the neighbouring smaller islands, and even on the mainland. It was also in this year that, the three first Christian Japanese, Angero and his two servants, after having been thoroughly instructed, were solemnly baptised on Whit-Sunday, by the Bishop Albuquerque, in the church of St. Paul whence, Angero took the name of *Paulo de Santa Fè*, in honor of the double name of the house. His first servant was called *Antonio*, in honor of the patron of the Portuguese nation, and the second, *João*, in honor of the Bishop who baptised him. Shortly after, Xavier, along with the three new Christians, and a priest and brother of his order, set out for Japan.

1552.—On the 2nd of December this year, Francis Xavier died in the island of Sancian, on the coast of China, whither he was going to preach the Gospel.

1553.—D. J. d'Albuquerque, first Bishop of Goa died, and the See remained seven years vacant.

1554.—On the 16th of March this year, the body of Francis Xavier, which had been transferred from Sancian to Malacca, was taken to Goa in triumph, attended by all the clergy and confraternities, by the Viceroy Noronha, the Senate, &c. It was deposited in the church of the college of St. Paul, and remained for a great number of years, exposed to the sight of the people, in a perfect state of preservation.

1557.—Pope Paul IV. erects Goa into a Metropolitan or Archiepiscopal See, and assigns it to two Suffragan Bishoprics; that of Cochin, the diocese of which was to begin at Cranganor, to comprehend the whole south of the peninsula, and all the Coast of Coromandel as far as the mouths of the Ganges, and to include all the Portuguese settlements; and east of that, the new diocese of Goa, which then comprehended the settlements north of Cranganor, and continued westward and southward to the Cape of Good Hope.*

---

* The other Suffragan Bishoprics of Goa, which were afterwards erected, were Macao for China and Japan, created in 1575, which still subsists. Funag, Capital of Bong, for all Japan, created in 1588, which is now extinct. Meliapor or St. Thomé created in 1606; and Nankin and Pekin, in China, created in 1690. All these Sees, as well as those of Cochin and Malacca, are still in existence, although they are vacant the greatest part of the time, or their titular prelates reside in Portugal; but they are administered in regard to their spiritual concerns, by priests named by the Archbishop of Goa, and delegated for that purpose by the King of Portugal as grand masters of the order of Christ, according to an agreement between the courts of Rome and Lisbon It is the same case with the Archbispopric of Cranganor, created at first at Angamale for the union of the Christian Malabars of St. Thomas, which became a simple bishopric in 1600; and nine years after, was raised anew to the dignity of an Archbishopric. and transferred to Cranganor, though without suffragans, but with the injunction of its prelates, assisting at the provincial councils of Goa, as constituting a part of that ecclesiastical province. Macao, is the only one of these Sees which is regularly filled, and which has a chapter, that administers during the vacancy It is likewise the only one which is now subject to the King of Portugal; but he is still considered as patron of all the other Sees; he names the prelates when he thinks proper and pays them.

1558.—Although the Chapter of Goa governed the diocese, according to the ancient statutes of the Catholic Church, the episcopal functions were performed by D. John Nugnes de Barreto, Patriarch of Ethiopia, and the first Bishop of the order of the Jesuits, who, not having been able to penetrate into Abyssinia, came to Goa, and fixed his residence in the small neighbouring island of Chorão, the inhabitants of which he was chiefly instrumental in converting to Christianity, and where, he founded a house of his order, which became afterwards the noviciate, and is now one of the two Archiepiscopal seminaries. The neighbouring island of Divar became soon likewise solely inhabited by Christians, and was divided into two parishes.

1560.—D. Gaspar de Leon Pereyra, canon of Evora, named and consecrated first Archbishop of Goa, arrives in that city ; and the first Episcopal ordination in India was performed in the church of St. Paul. The new Archbishop, assisted by the patriarch of Ethiopia, and the Bishop of Malacca, consecrated Father Melchior Camero, a Jesuit, under the title of Bishop of Nicea, and as 2nd coadjutor of the aforesaid patriarch. But, as he never was able to go to Abyssinia,* he became first Bishop of China and Japan, and died at Macao after he had resigned his See. On the evening of the same day and in the same church in the presence of the four prelates, 409 persons received baptism, chiefly from the peninsula of Salsette, on the south of the island of Goa. Until then, there was, in that peninsula, but one single church and mission house in the fort of Rachol, which, after having been given to the Jesuits, became of late the chief Archiepiscopal seminary on account of its more healthy situa-

* Andrew Oviedo, who had been named the first coadjutor of the patriarch, and who had been consecrated along with him at Lisbon, was the only Bishop who went to Abyssinia and resided there several years.

tion than that of Chorão. In the course of less than fifty years, all the inhabitants of Salsette embraced Christianity, and 28 parishes were erected therein. In this same year was founded the too celebrated tribunal of the Inquisition, against which so much has been written and said. Though we are very far from justifying its proceedings, we are at the same time obliged to declare, that many falsehoods and exaggerations have been advanced respecting it. It must be owned, it is true, first, that this tribunal, both in Spain and Portugal, greatly degenerated from its original institution; secondly, that many of its forms were extremely vicious and cruel; though it might be observed at the same time, particularly, as to the tortures it inflicted, that it had them in common with all the civil tribunals existing in the time it was erected; and thirdly, that the governors, powerful men, and the corrupted part of the clergy, took too often advantage of the vicious way in which justice was administered in that tribunal, to satisfy their private vengeance and hatred, as is evident in the case of Dellon, and of several other persons whom he mentions. But, on the other hand, it must be confessed, that the cruelties of that tribunal have been greatly exaggerated; whereas, we see in the first place, that the Inquisitions, during the greatest part of the time, sincerely desired to save the lives of their prisoners, and that at every *Acto de Fè*, of the great number of the accused and supposed convicts, very few suffered death, and almost all of these were strangled before they were burnt; secondly, that the greatest care was taken of the lives, health, and cleanliness of the prisoners, at a time when all the public prisons, in almost all Christian countries, were kept in a most wretched and inhumane state; thirdly, that the rigours of the Inquisition were never exercised but against Christians, and not even against individuals out of the Catholic communion, unless they relapsed, and that they never forced any one either to embrace Christianity or to become a Catholic.* Thus much have we said to shew our entire impartiality, but by no means to approve the institution itself, nor to excuse it from all that has been advanced against it; it is merely to correct false and unwarranted statements, which can have no other effect than that of leading the readers into erroneous opinions, and of propagating falsehood, a thing always very blameable, whatever may be the intentions of the authors of it.

1567.—The first Provincial Council of Goa, held, presided by Don Gaspar de Leon è Pereira, Archbishop. There were besides him, Don Fr. George de Themudo, of the order of St. Dominic, the Bishop of Cochin, the deputy of the Bishop of Malacca, the Vicar General of Mosambique, and the heads of the Monasteries in Goa. Thirty-eight decrees, regarding church discipline, were pronounced in this assembly.

1568.—Don Gaspar Leon resigns his See, and is succeeded by Don Fr. George Themudo, who is transferred from Cochin.

1572.—The foundation of the Monastery of the Augustinians, on the Mount of the Rosary is laid. This order became the 4th in Goa; this same year Pope Gregory XIII. grants to the Bishops of Cochin, the right of administering the Archbishopric of Goa, during its vacancy.

1573.—On the death of Fr. George de Themudo, second Archbishop of Goa, Don Gaspar de Leon obtains new Bulls, and assumes the Archiepiscopal functions.

* All this is clearly proved by Dellon's own account of the Inquisition of Goa, though that very account is so often cited as a monument of shame to that tribunal.

1575.—Second Provincial Council of Goa held, composed of Don Gaspar de Leon, President, Don Henry de Tavra, the Bishop of Cochin, the deputy of the Bishop of Malacca, the grand inquisitor, and sixteen secular or regular Priests being the deputies of the chapters of Goa and Cochin, the Provincials and heads of Monasteries, and the Vicars General, &c. There were three sessions; in the first, were pronounced three decrees; in the second twelve; and in the third and last, eighteen.

1578.—D. F. Henry de Tavra, of the order of St. Dominic, Bishop of Cochin, succeeds, in the Archiepiscopal dignity, Don Gaspar de Leon Pereira, deceased.

1580.—The convent of St. Augustine is rebuilt in its present state, being now the finest in Goa.

1583.—D. Fr. Vincent de Fonçeca of the order of St. Dominic, becomes Archbishop of Goa.

1584.—The foundation is laid of the professed house of the Jesuits, the church of which was called *Bom-Jesus*, to which the body of St. Francis Xavier was transferred, and where it remains to this day.

1585.—The third Provincial Council of Goa held, composed of D. Vincent de Fonçeca, Archbishop, President, D. Fr. Matthew de Medina, Bishop of Cochin, the famous Mar Abraham, the Syrian Bishop of Angamale, the deputy of the Bishop of Malacca, the deputies from the three chapters of Goa, Cochin, and Malacca and several other secular and regular priests.—There were five sessions and eighty decrees issued; ten of these related to the Archbishopric of Angamale, and to the Christians of St. Thomas or of Malabar. Mar Abraham made his abjuration of the Nestorian heresy, which he again professed several times, though he protested, on his death-bed, that he died a Catholic, of his own free will; for he was not then under the power of the Portuguese.*

1582.—D. Fr. Matthew of Medina, of the order of Christ, Bishop of Cochin, becomes Archbishop of Goa.

1592.—Fourth Provincial Council of Goa is held, in which the Archbishop as usual presided, and sixteen decrees are issued.

1595.—D. Fr. Alexius de Menezes, of the order of St. Augustine, becomes Archbishop of Goa.

1599.—The famous Synod of Adampier, on the coast of Malabar, for the reunion of the Christians of St. Thomas, is held by Archbishop Menezes; concerning this Synod much has been written, but as the subject is foreign to our purpose, we will say nothing about it.

1600.—Before this year, the second convent of the Franciscans was founded without the city, in the eastern suburb near the river; it was called the convent of the Mother of God, and in the following century, was separated from the congregation of the observentine Franciscans, and incorporated with that of the reformed Franciscans, called also *Recollects;* thus it became the head of a new order in Goa and the residence of a provincial, having several other convents in India dependent on it. These monks are improperly called *Capuchy* in Goa, being quite different from the Capuchins.

1602.—Foundation is laid of the college, for persons entering into the order of St. Augustine, close to the great convent with which it communicates by an arch

* This prelate is the competitor and successor of Mar Joseph, both of whom went several times to Europe, either forcibly or of their own accord, in order to get themselves confirmed in their Sees, and Mar Joseph is the man, whom, Yeates and some other English author pretend to have been arrested by order of Archbishop Menezes, who, at that time, was only five years old.

over the street. The college of St. Thomas of Aquinas for the Dominicans, in the western suburb of St. Peter or Pannely, close to the shore, was founded shortly after this period, as well as that of St. Bonaventure for the Franciscans of the observance, on the shore, within the limits of the city, and at a very little distance west of the convent. That of St. Rock for the Jesuits, on Mount Rosary, close to the church of that name, has existed since several years.

1606.—Fifth Provincial Council of Goa, presided by Archbishop Menezes, who (as his successors have done) entitles himself *Primate of the East;* one hundred and forty-nine decrees are formed in four sessions ; this is the last Catholic Council held in India.

1607.—Foundation laid of the convent of the discalceated or barefooted Carmelites near that of St. Dominic.

1610.—Assembly of Bishops in Goa, presided by the Archbishop, for assigning the respective limits of the four dioceses of Goa, Cranganor, Cochin and Meliapor.

1613.—D. Alexius de Menezes is transferred to the Archbishopric of Braga, in Portugal. This prelate issued from one of the noblest houses of Portugal, and notwithstanding all the calumnies advanced against him by the English writers, he was most virtuous and exemplary, and very humane in all his conduct. It is false that he used violence at the Synod of Adampiere, to force the Malabar Christians to unite with the Catholic Church; all the authentic records of that assembly prove, that he only made use of gentle and persuasive means for that purpose. Some acts of violence by the Portuguese agents may have been committed, both before and after him, but they are not to be imputed to him. It is equally false, that, followed by the officers of the Inquisition, he went armed with fire and sword, to compel the inhabitants of Salsette to embrace the Christian religion. The Jesuits converted a great part of them by the usual and most laudable means; but in order, as they thought, the better to detach the remainder of the inhabitants from the worship of idols, they destroyed all the temples and pagodas. This however had a contrary effect; and the Pagans, exasperated at this circumstance, rose up in arms, murdered five Jesuits, and several Portuguese. The Governor then felt himself obliged to use arms likewise to reduce the rebels; and of course did not afterwards permit the temples to be rebuilt. But in all this the Archbishop had nothing to do, and what is certainly better proved, are the good works and the pious establishments of Goa, of which he is the founder. It was he who induced the confraternity of *Misericordia* to build three houses, one for aged and infirm men, one for widows, and one for young girls, who, after a suitable instruction afforded to them, were at liberty to marry, and received a settlement from the funds of the house. These institutions still subsist notwithstanding the reduced state of Goa; he also founded the monastery of the nuns of St. Monica, of the order of St. Augustine on Mount Rosary, near the great Augustinian convent; and lastly, erected another parochial church in the centre of the city, not far from the cathedral, which he dedicated to St. Alexius, whose name he bore. Since the division of Goa into four parishes, under the Governor Sousa and the first Bishop Albuquerque, three other parishes and an extra parochial chapel have been erected. They were, the parochial church of St. Thomas, the apostle, in the south eastern part of the town; that of the Blessed Trinity, on the south; that of St. Peter, in the western suburb, called Pannely, near the Dominican college of St. Thomas Aquinas;

and the extra parochial chapel of the five wounds of our Saviour, in the King's arsenal. So that, from this time, the city and suburbs contained eight parishes and one extra parochial church, which still subsist, though, with hardly any parishioners, except the two churches of the Blessed Trinity and of St. Alexius, which are abandoned and in ruins since more than fifty years. Archbishop Menezes, soon after his removal to Braga, became Viceroy of Portugal for Philip III. King of Spain, and died, as he had lived, in 1617.

1616.—Don Fr. Christopher Sa de Lisboa, of the order of St. Jerom, and Bishop of Malacca, is transferred to the Archiepiscopal See of Goa. It was this Archbishop who began the rebuilding of the cathedral of Goa.

1629.—Don Fr. Sebastian of St. Peter, of the order of St. Augustine, first Bishop of Meliapor and afterwards Bishop of Cochin, became Archbishop of Goa, and completes the building of the cathedral in its present state, and consecrates it anew. He dies in the year following.

1631.—Don Fr. Emmanuel de Telles, of the order of St. Dominic, dies on his way to Goa, whither he was going to take possession of the Archbishopric.

1635.—Don Fr. Francis de Martyribus, of the order of St. Francis, Archbishop of Goa, who died in 1652.

1659.—The church, called the Miraculous Cross, which had been built ever since 1608, and which belongs to the Augustinians, is rebuilt in its present state, on a hill south of the city near the parochial church of *Luz*, and commands a beautiful view, not only of all the town, but of all the island and harbour of Goa.

1672.—Don Fr. Christopher de Silveira, of the order of St. Augustine, named and consecrated Archbishop of Goa, arrives and takes possession of the See, which had been vacant for 20 years. It was a little before the arrival of the Archbishop, that the French Physician Dellon was committed to the Inquisition, of which he afterwards gave an account, which, though it contains some expressions unwarrantable for a Catholic, and which savour of his private resentment, is nevertheless far from being too exaggerated; and even on many points rather justifies than accuses that tribunal. He had been arrested ostensibly for some bold and even erroneous assertions, though excusable in a layman, who is not so much obliged to know the mysteries of divinity; but the chief cause, however, of his misfortune, was the jealousy of a Governor of Daman, who misrepresented his case.

1675.—D. Fr. Antony Brandon, of the Cistercian order, becomes Archbishop of Goa, and dies three years after.

1675.—D. Emmanuel de Sousa de Menezes, a secular priest, becomes Archbishop of Goa.

1675.—D. Albert of St. Gonzalo, canon regular of St. Augustine, is Archbishop of Goa.

1691.—D. Augustine de Annunciação, of the order of Christ, is consecrated Archbishop the preceding year, arrives in Goa, and dies in 1712.

Before the end of this century, was founded the convent of the Theatins or of St. Cajetan, by the Italians of that order. The church which they rebuilt according to the model of that of St. Peter at Rome though small, is the most perfect edifice in Goa. It was originally the chapel of the Viceroy, being situated, as well as the convent, near the palace. Some time after the beginning of the 18th century, was founded, the convent of the Brothers of Charity, or St. John of God, to whose care the hospitals were committed.

1716.—D. Sebastian de Andrade Passanha, secular priest, Archbishop of Goa ; he afterwards resigns his See.

1721.—D. Ignatius of St. Theresa, canon regular of St. Augustine, Archbishop of Goa, he is afterwards transferred to the Bishopric of Algarves in Portugal.

1741.—D. Fr. Eugenius Inguiros, of the order of St. Jerom, Bishop of Macao, is transferred to Goa, but dies on his way to that city.

1742.—D. Fr. Laurence de Santa Maria, is named Archbishop, but never comes to Goa.

1750.—D. Antony Taveira de Neiva, of the military order of Santyago, Archbishop of Goa.

1761.—The Jesuits are expelled from all the dominions of the King of Portugal. Their professed house of *Bom-Jesus* is given to the Italian missionaries of St. Vincent of Paul, known better under the name of Lazarists, there to hold the episcopal seminary. The house of the noviciate of Chorão, on the island of that name, is given to the priests of the congregation of St. Philip of Neri, chiefly natives and descendants of Brahmins ; as well as the house of the Jesuits at Rachol, in Salsette, now the chief episcopal seminary. The colleges and churches of St. Paul and of St. Rock, are abandoned and suffered to go to ruins as they are now seen in. The chief house of the priests of St. Philip of Neri, had been founded some time before, near the church of the Miraculous Cross, which had belonged formerly to the Augustinians, as we have said. They built a large convent near it, which is now one of the finest, richest, and the healthiest in Goa. They obtained likewise possession of the ancient convent of the barefooted Carmelites, who, since about 1739 were expelled from Goa, on account of the dissension that had arisen between that order, supported by the Propaganda, and the Archbishops of Goa, concerning the spiritual jurisdiction of the island of Bombay, which is not yet entirely settled. Their convent became the private college of the Philippians or congregationers as they are called. Those monks, who are now all of the Brahminical caste, are very rich ; and to their care are intrusted not only the two episcopal seminaries, as we have said, but likewise the missions of Ceylon in the diocese of Cochin.

1773.—D. Francis al Assumptione Britto, of the order of St. Augustine, becomes Archbishop of Goa. This prelate, who was the true creature of the famous Marquis of Pombal, gave great offence by his innovations. Though a monk, he rejected the title of *Frè* according to the custom of the Portuguese prelates. He despoiled the library of Goa of its most precious manuscripts and other works, which he sent to Lisbon. He was disliked generally by all his clergy and the people at large. After the disgrace of the Marquis of Pombal, he was suspended by Pope Pius VI. along with three others of the Portuguese dominions, and died in 1780.

1780.—D. Fr. Emmanuel of Santa Catharina, barefooted Carmelite, is named Archbishop of Goa. It is related of this prelate, that, shortly after his arrival in India, some Carmelites of the Bombay Mission, presented themselves before him and said, that they hoped that since his Excellency was of their order, matters should soon and easily come to a mutual and happy conclusion ; but he shrewdly answered : "*Reverend Fathers, before I became a Carmelite, I was a Portuguese.*" In truth, the dissension, far from becoming subsided, was renewed with more warmth than ever, under Governor Duncan, in Bombay. About 1798, by the exertion of Michael de Lima, a powerful native, held in great estimation by the English, and who declared himself for the jurisdiction of the Archbishop, it was terminated, by the division of the four parishes of the Island, then existing, between the Bishop Vicar Apostolic of Mogul, head of the Carmelite Mission, and the Archbishop, who, however, protests to this day against this act, though he submits to it as approved of by the Pope. Fr. Emmanuel of Santa Catharina was a simple, but holy prelate. He was notwithstanding what has been said of him, much attached to his order ; and not being able to restore to them their convent, he erected a society of priests of the third order of the Carmelites, who pronounce only simple vows, like the priests of St. Philip of Neri, but who wear the Carmelite habit. He built them a convent and a church, called *Chimbel*, near the church of St. Barbara, between the villages of Ribandar and Pangi. As the convents of the Theatins, or St. Cajetan and that of the priests of St. Philip Neri, received exclusively natives of the Brahminical caste, that of *Chimbel* was consecrated entirely for the second native caste of Goa called *Chardos*.

1783.—The body of St. Francis Xavier, in the church of *Bom-Jesus*, which had been before constantly exposed to view, and which was afterwards exhibited only on certain occasions, was exposed for the last time in this year ; ever since which it has been locked up in its beautiful brazen shrine, under three keys, one of which is kept by the Archbishop, the other by the Senate, and the third is at Lisbon.

1790.—The Italian Lazarists, who, since the expulsion of the Jesuits, were in possession of the house and church of *Bom-Jesus*, and of the Archiepiscopal Seminary, are expelled from Goa, according to some regulations contrary to their statutes, which the Governor and the Archbishop would impose upon them. The house and church were then intrusted to the care of a secular priest, with the title of Administrator, and with sufficient revenues. This place is commonly occupied by one of the canons of the Cathedral.

1812.—D. Fr. Emmanuel de Santo Galdino, a reformed Franciscan, or Recollect, of the province of Arrabida, in Portugal, was named Bishop of Macao in 1803, and transferred thence to Goa as coadjutor, in 1805, he arrives in Goa the following year, and succeeds to the Archbishopric on the death of his predecessor, which happened this year, on the 10th of February.

S. IV.—*Topographical and Statistical description of the City and Island of Goa in their present state, as likewise of the two provinces of Salsette and Bardes, and of the new surrounding provinces.*

The actual extent and the state of Goa.

The present city of Goa, improperly called Old Goa by foreigners, was built by the Mahometans of Onor, in 1479, as we have said before, in Latitude 15° 31' N. and Longitude E. of London 73° 55', on the northern shore of the island that bears its name, and which is also called Tissuary, or improperly a river, but which is in fact an arm of the sea, separating the said island, on the south, from the peninsula of Bardes, and the islands of Chorão and Divar on the north. The city is directly opposite this last mentioned island, and of course by more than one-half nearer to the eastern than to the western extremity of the island of Goa. Its centre is about six miles distant from the ocean. Although now almost destitute of houses and inhabitants, as we shall see, it nevertheless comprehends the usual space of ground or extent, as it did in its greatest splendour. Its length from east to west, is about a mile and a quarter, not including the suburbs of Dowji on the east, and of St. Peter or Pannely on the west. It extends in breadth, from the shore or quay, up to the top of the hill, on which the church of *Luz* is situated, about three-quarters of a mile, presenting, therefore, an extent of three and three-quarter square miles. The suburb of Lower Dowji or of St. Lucia, on the east, is very trifling, containing only about fifty houses on the two sides of the street; but that of St. Peter or Pannely, on the west, is much more considerable, though consisting of but a single row of houses, facing the shore and the north, and extending very nearly from the city to the village of Ribandar; which last communicating with Pangi, it follows, that the whole road, between Goa and the new capital Pangi, is wholly bordered with houses, and is the best inhabited part of the island.

Goa never had any walls on the east and south; those that begin in the suburb of Little Dowji, and which extend along the eastern shore of the island, were extended, as we have said, by the Viceroy Antonio de Noronha their founder, to defend the weak part of the island, and never were considered as the ramparts of the city. The wall from the church and the gate of St. James or St. Yago, had been continued, not along the rest of the shore, but in a western direction, until the summit of the hill or mountain south of that of the Rosary, or of the Augustinians; and thence it took a southern direction, and formed the true limits of the city, down to the shore, separating it thus from the suburb of St. Peter or Pannely. This latter part of the wall is now entirely destroyed, but a ditch with which it seems to have been fortified, on that side, is still to be seen, the water flowing down from the hills to the sea. There is still a bridge over it, by which the suburb communicates with the city ; and on the side of the latter, low walls of private inclosures extend along the said ditch. The southern part of the wall is also destroyed as far as a gate about a quarter of a mile S. W. of the church of *Luz* ; the gate still stands, as well as the three others along the eastern shore, viz : St. Yago, that of the Dry Passage, and that of Dowji. Within this large inclosure, are comprehended, the villages and churches of St. Joseph, or Upper Dowji, St. Blasius, St. Yago or St. James, Carambolim, St. Simon, Asocim, and Corlim ; all these villages are very small, and cannot be considered as part of the city, nor included in its population, except the churches, convents, and other public edifices, of which we will speak presently. There is not a single decent looking house in good repair in all the city. Some very insignificant ones and fast decaying, are only to be seen, towards the centre, between the houses of *Misericordia* and the Bazaar. All the rest is a vast solitude, a very few wretched huts being only to be found, and at very great distances from each other. Nevertheless, the chief streets and public squares, are still distinguishable, and the greatest part of them are still bordered on the two sides with low and mouldering stone walls. In certain places, these walls are perforated and a hut is raised behind of mud against it which serves to lodge a miserable family, to whom, the hole serves as an exterior door. The greatest part of the ground within the city, out of the streets, is covered with cocoanut trees, which afford a revenue to the churches, convents, and to a few individuals. The houses of the suburb of St. Lucia or Lower Dowji are somewhat a little better, and a part of them are inhabited by Mahometans and Hindoos ; as for those of Pannely or St. Peter, many are very elegantly constructed and are in the best state of repair and probably in as good a condition as when the city was well inhabited. One coming from Pangi, and seeing a-far off the numerous churches of Goa, with their towers and spires, and the handsome and neat houses of Pannely, would really think, that he is going to enter a superb metropolis; but he is strangely disappointed, as soon as he approaches, finding himself suddenly transported into the midst of a desert. The houses of Goa, as we may judge from ancient accounts, and from those of Pangi and Pannely, were elegant and spacious, generally of only one story above the ground floor; all, yearly white-washed, and many of them with balconies, having the door and window frames painted green, and instead of panes of glass, small pieces of mother of pearls, about two inches long and one broad, are joined together with small thin plates of lead. But all those ornaments would be in vain sought for now in Pannely, except, in the churches and convents. Some of the streets must have been also paved; for Dellon, in his account of the Inquisition, complains bitterly of the sharpness of the stones which made his feet bleed, when he was conducted in procession to the *Acto de Fé*. Some remains of this pavement are in fact still to be seen towards the centre of the town; as for the rest, the soil being sandy and stooping, the streets must always have been pretty cleanly kept. They were long, but neither very wide nor very straight; and as all the houses had spacious gardens attached to them, the number of streets could not be very great, and therefore the communications between the different parts of the town, must have been very long and tedious, which is of course still the case.

Population of Goa.

Goa is now divided into five parishes, within the limits of the city, including, however, St. Lucia or Lower Dowji; half of which, with its church, is reckoned within the suburbs. Though no regular account of the population has been taken, yet we may approximate to a true estimation by the following informations, which may be relied upon as correct.

The number of Easter Communicants, in the five parishes, is as follows, as extracted from the parochial register:—

	Easter Communicants.
In the Cathedral	110
In the Rosary	6
In Luz	8
In St. Thomas	25
In St. Lucia or Dowji	56
Total	205

To this number again, about one-third of it must be added for the children and servants, who do not all reside in the city during the whole year and for some few Pagans and Mahometans	68
Consequently, the total number of lay inhabitants of both sexes, with their children and servants in the city of Goa, and the suburb or Lower Dowji, amounts to about	273
The number of secular clergymen residing or supposed by their functions to reside in Goa, amounts to	70
Number of Friars or Monks, either professed, or Novices or lay Brothers, not including those of the convents of *Mater Dei* or reformed Franciscans, nor those of *Chimbel* or of the Third Order of the Carmelites as being out of the city amounts to about	170

Nuns of the Monastery of St. Monica 30

Servants and slaves attached to the convents of both sexes, (as one is allowed to every priest or ancient professed in every convent, and a girl at least for each nun in the monastery), and the servants of the secular priests. 300

People of both sexes living in the three-houses of *Misericordia* and the Hospitals within the bounds of the city, including the servants and slaves 200

People employed in the Arsenal, in the extra parochial church of the Five Wounds, situated within the establishment 100

Total number of persons residing within the limits of the city, and the suburb of St. Lucia or Lower Dowji........................ 1,143

The suburb of Pannely, constituting the parish of St. Peter, counts fifteen hundred communicants at Easter........................ 1,500

And children, servants, Mahometans, Hindoos, and strangers. 500

— 2,000

Total... 3,143

Thus the city of Goa, with its suburb, must contain about 3,200 inhabitants, nearly two-thirds of whom reside in the suburb of Pannely or St. Peter.

Civil Edifices of Goa.

They consist now of the palace of the Viceroy, the Senate house, the arsenal, the old custom house, the old town hospital. To these must be added, the bazaar, the slaughter house, and the wharf or landing place; most of these are now abandoned and in ruins.

The palace founded by Albuquerque, but enlarged and rebuilt several times since, was a large and stately edifice, in form of our L. bordering on the wharf or water side. It was built entirely of free stones, and the roof tiled. Under it is an arch way leading from the interior of the city to the river. In this passage is still to be seen the statue of Vasco de Gama. This palace is said to have been very richly adorned in the inside; but for nearly two centuries, the viceroys and governors have resided in the powder house or *Casa de Polvora*, in the suburb of Pannely, thus called, from a neighbouring gun powder manufactory still existing, but the governor held his solemn audiences on festivals and on particular occasions in the great hall of the palace, until as late as 1812; it has, however, been ever since entirely abandoned, and the roof is for the greatest part, sunk in, though the walls, which are very broad and solid, are still entire.

The senate of the city of Goa, use to hold its meetings in the building, in front of the Cathedral, which is also of free stone and sufficiently spacious. But this house serves now as an hospital to the sick of the *casas de Misericordia*, and is going fast to ruins. The senate holds now its sessions in another smaller stone building, apparently new, situate on the north of the same square and in front of the Inquisition. It is a very neat but insignificant edifice.

The arsenal is a collection of several houses connected with one another, and forming an irregular square like the shape of a cloister. In this building were, and are still, made or received from Europe, all the war and naval stores. There are still about one hundred individuals, occupied not only in objects of that kind, but in other public works: some are convicts and others are entertained and paid for their labour. There is a chapel in the N. E. corner, bearing the name of the Five Wounds of Christ ; it is an extra parochial, and the chaplain thereof exercises all the parochical functions over the people of the establishment. All the buildings of the arsenal are in good repair ; a guard comes every day from Pangi, to maintain the police of the place, and is changed every morning.

The old Custom-House was a very insignificant building on the wharf, near the Gardens and enclosure of the convent of St. Cajetan. It is now falling into ruins, having been abandoned for above thirty years and the officers of that department having been removed to Pangi.

The Royal Hospital used to be formerly close to the Arsenal on the eastern side, and near the chapel of St. Catherine ; but it was removed to the Powder-house or *Casa de Polvora*, in Pannely when the Viceroy Don Emmanuel de Saldanha d'Albuquerque, Count of Ega, transferred his residence from that place to Pangi, in 1759, as we have mentioned. There now remains no trace of the ancient hospital, the space which it occupied being now included within the exterior walls of the Arsenal.

The city hospital in the south eastern part of the town and parish of the Blessed Trinity, is now almost deserted; there are only some few beggars residing therein, and the house is rapidly decaying; it was small and had nothing remarkable.

The bazar, built in the form of a cloister, in the centre of the town, is very mean; so is the slaughter house, contiguous to these establishments, which are now merely nominal; the buildings are become the retreat of beggars, thieves, and the few native travellers that pass through Goa.

The wharf or quay, is a noble work, being entirely supported with a wall of free stone on the river side; it extends from the eastern house to the Arsenal, and is ornamented with a double row of trees; from it, one has a full view of the town, rising on the hills above, in the form of an amphitheatre. This quay is still very well preserved, and there are two stone stairs to go down to the boats.

We must add to the buildings we have already noticed, the Royal Hospital, or *Casa de Polvora*, in the suburb of Pannely, which is in very good repair, sufficiently large and facing the water. The sick therein, amounting generally to about sixty, are now much better taken care of than formerly. The Brothers of Charity, or of St. John of God, are charged with the care of this hospital, and six of them always remain in it. Near this, is the gun-powder manufactory, which, is still kept up.

The hospital of St. Lazarus, at the eastern extremity of Goa, was formerly confined only to Lepers ; but now the poor are all admitted in it. A secular priest superintends the establishment, and officiates as their chaplain ; all those who are able to pay are admitted into the King's hospital, along with the sick soldiers and sailors. The hospital of St. Lazarus, was that which St. Francis Xavier affectionated most, and wherein he generally passed the night, in order that he might help and serve the sick.

The Cathedral of Goa, and the Archiepiscopal Palaces.

The Cathdral, or rather Metropolitan Church of Goa, was founded soon after the conquest by the Portuguese as the first parochial church of the town, and it became a cathedral in 1534, as we have said. It was originally dedicated only to St. Catherine, whose name alone is mentioned in the Pope's bulls of erection. But it afterwards assumed, as patron and patroness, St. Peter and the Blessed Virgin, so that it has now one patron and two patronesses. The festival of the Assumption on the 15th of August, is that celebrated in honour of the Virgin Mary in her character of patroness. It was enlarged and re-built in its present state by the Archbishop Christopher de Sa, or of Lisbon, who took possession of the See in 1616, and the work being completed, it was consecrated anew in 1630, by the Archbishop Sebastian of St. Peter, as we have stated in the preceding paragraph.

This church, situated on the west side of the great square, is a building after the modern style, with little display of exterior ornaments, except in the front, which is in itself very simple, but very decent; it lies from east to west, and contrary to the common practice of building Christian churches, the choir is turned in the latter direction. It is about 200 feet in length, and the nave or body of the church is about 80 broad, divided into three naves by two rows of pillars, and not including a row of chapels on either side; the transept, forming across with the nave, is about 130 feet in length, and 50 in breadth. The choir, raised only three or four steps, is of the same breadth as the middle nave, that is about 45 feet. It is not round at the end as customary, but represents an oblong square; there are no side aisles around it. The height, to the top of the vault of the whole edifice, is about 40 feet. The church is only lighted by the windows above the pillars, and those of the choir and of the transept which are much elevated from the ground, as almost the whole church is surrounded with other buildings adhering to the walls thereof, except in the front. The altar is situated at the extremity of the choir. The altar piece is well carved and gilt, consisting of three rows of niches one above the other, and adorned with pillars, pillasters, and other ornaments. The niches in the middle row, are for the statues of the three patrons, the Virgin, St. Peter and St. Catherine. However, the whole bears now an appearance of antiquity, and the gilding is far from being fresh. The stalls, or seats of the canons, occupy the two sides of the choir from the steps of the sanctuary to the railings that separate it from the nave. The Archbishop's throne is on the gospel or southern side. On the opposite side, over the stalls, are two organs in the galleries and a pulpit, into all of which they enter by doors in the walls, to which they ascend by stairs from within the vestry. One of the organs is for daily use, and the other for festivals, but none of these has any thing remarkable in it. There are fourteen other altars, of which four are against the western walls of the transept, two on either side, and the rest in the chapels, on the two sides of the nave ; and at the entrance there are baptismal fonts, as the church is at the same time parochial. The statues, though all gilt, are very badly, or at least, ordinarily carved, and there are very few insignificant paintings. All the windows give light through small panes of mother of pearls, as we have mentioned, which cast a gloomy shade over the inside of the church. The front is ornamented with three doors, a fine flight of steps descending to the square, and some niches ; it is surrounded with a square tower, in which there is a tolerable range of bells. The vestry is on the south side of the choir, and communicates with the transept. Its treasure, vases, reliquaries, and priests' vestments, are all very rich ; but the latter, and all the silk and embroidered ornaments bear now an appearance of oldness, but not so much however as in the other churches, or even those in the rich convents.

The clergy of this church is composed as follows: I have set down the amount of every benefice or living and summed up the whole, to shew the amount of the revenues of the church.

	Goa Rs. per Ann.	
The Achbishop of Goa, primate of the East	8,000	8,000
The Dean	500	500
The four other dignitaries, (*Cantor*, Treasurer, Archdeacon and Scholastic,) each	300	1,200
Ten Canons or Prebendaries, each...	250	2,500
Four Semi-prebendaries, each ...	140	650
Two Quartenarians, each	130	260
Twelve Priests' Chaplains, each ...	90	1,080
		14,100
Four Vestrymen, Priests or Laymen, each	60	240
Twelve Clingers, Priests or Laymen, each	48	576
Six Singing Boys, each	38	216
One Parish Priest, bearing the title of Curate (*Cura*)	180	180
Three Assistants, each	90	270
60 Members. Total revenue of the Cathedral...		15,582
But exclusive of the Archbishop's income of		8,000
There remains for all the rest of the Clergy		7,582

This must appear exceedingly small to Europeans, and chiefly to English readers; but it is much in proportion to the state of property in the country, where, a half *pardou* or quarter rupee is supposed to suffice for the decent maintenance of a single person. The clergy are in general paid from the royal treasury, as is the case throughout all the Portuguese dominions, ever since the King has obtained from the Pope the right of receiving the tithes himself.

Divine Service is performed twice a day in the Cathedral ; in the morning the canons and others assemble at eight, and Matins, Lauds, and Prime, are sung on festivals, and read on the other days of the year. Every day, on festivals, and on Sundays or week days, Terce is sung, and the High Mass celebrated, after which Sext is sung or read. The canons, who do not reside in the town, have their dinner carried to their residence, as either in the neighbouring palace or convents or in some friend's house. At half-past two, they go to the choir again and recite or sing None, Vespers and Compline. Sermons are preached on festivals, in Lent, and in Advent. All the priests of the cathedral say their Masses privately at the different altars, either before the morning service, or during the performance of it, absenting themselves by two or three at a time.

The Archbishop officiates on Holy Thursday, for the consecration of the holy Oil, and on Easter, Christmas, *Corpus Christi,* and St. Peter's day; and the present prelate generally preaches the sermon on Good Friday, but he seldom attends the choir the rest of the year, as he lives in Pannely. When the Archbishop officiates, he is attended by the four first dignitaries, who sit on each side of him on his throne. The fifth dignitary, or in his absence, the senior canon, stands as deacon, and the youngest of all as sub-deacon; in case of the forced absence of some of the dignitaries, the canons supply their place in right of seniority, but it is always the youngest, or rather last promoted present, who stands sub-deacon. The Dean officiates on certain festivals and on those assigned to the Archbishop, when he is absent. All the other dignitaries and canons officiate each their week; and whenever they are prevented from so doing it is the part of the Semi-prebendaries and Quartenarians to supply their place, having no week of their own. The chaplains and singers are merely for the choir. All the members of the clergy belonging to the cathedral, unless for legitimate causes are obliged to assist every day at the office, except during a certain period of vacation, which they all have, but successively and by rotation. The two canons or dignitaries alone, whom the Archbishop employs in his palace, are exempted from the daily office, but not from officiating during their week.

The *Cura* or parish priest of the cathedral and his three assistants, though proportionally better paid than the vicars, are not the better off for that, as the *casual* of the parish is very insignificant.

All the members of the clergy belonging to the cathedral, except the dean, who is named by the King, are at the nomination of the Governor or Viceroy, upon the presentation of the Archbishop; but he can reject those presentations, and even name himself, provided the Archbishop can prove no canonical impediment; they are, however, both obliged in promoting them to Dignitaries, Prebendaries, and Semi and Quarter Prebendaries, to have regard to the distinction of seniority, by which all ascend regularly, unless there be some grave objections to their promotion. All European Portuguese, however, that are secular clergymen in India, unless for any canonical impediment, are promoted to the first place vacant, in the chapter of the cathedral, either of dignitary or prebendary.* Adjoining the cathedral on the north side is the archiepiscopal palace, but since several years the prelate resides in that of St. Peter, and remains in this only during the four last days of the Holy Week, and some canons alone occupy it. It is a pretty large but old and gloomy building.†

The palace of St. Peter or Pannelly, in the suburb of that name, about a quarter of a mile from the city, is in a much better situation, on the gentle ascent of a hill, commanding a sight of the water and of the opposite island, but rather at some distance, being separated from the great causeway by gardens. Its front represents a story above the ground floor, and the stair is very fine. But owing to the unevenness of the ground, there is but a ground floor in the inside, forming a square cloister with the front. The inside is very becomingly decorated, chiefly the great hall, wherein the Archbishop receives his visitors. In the outer hall are pictures, at full length and as large as life, of all the Archbishops of Goa to the present one. When the Archbishop goes out on festivals and public purposes, he is always preceded by a young clergyman, bearing a large silver cross. Like the Governor, he has only two sorts of conveyances, a *Palki* after the Bombay fashion, and a boat suitably painted and ornamented. In the first case, the clergyman, bearing the cross, goes in an open *Palki* before him, and, in the second, the cross is fixed to the prow of the boat.

---

* At present (1829) there are but the Dean and the Archdeacon who are Europeans, and they are the only secular clergymen natives of Portugal in the whole diocese.

† The last Archbishop, Fre Emanuel á Santa Catharina, constantly resided in this palace and died therein, though he used occasionally to take up his abode in that of St. Agnes. On the arrival of his coadjutor the present Archbishop, (Emanuel á Santo Galdino) this latter palace was allotted to him, as that of Pannely was out of repair, and uninhabited since several years. However, it having been since repaired, he transferred his residence thither, and continued to live in it after he became titular Archbishop, by the death of his predecessor.

There is a third archiepiscopal palace or country residence of the Archbishop, in the parish of St. Agnes about a mile west of Pangi.

The Collegiate, and Parish Churches of Goa.

There were, as we have said, since 1600, eight parochial churches and one extra parochial, in Goa and its suburbs, viz : the Cathedral, the Rosary, *Luz*, the Blessed Trinity, St. Thomas, St. Alexius, St. Lucia, St. Peter, and the Five Wounds in the Arsenal. The churches of the Blessed Trinity and of St. Alexius, are now in ruins and abandoned, and have been thus, since very near a century. Of the cathedral we have already spoken. The church of Our Lady of the Rosary, the third, or at least one of the oldest churches in Goa, is situated on the mountain to which it gives its name, at the back of the ruined Jesuit convent of St. Rock, and is very well seen from the suburb of St. Peter. The building has all the signs of antiquity and approaching ruin; it is not large, and there are now but six communicants in this church, in which Mass is said only on Sundays and festivals. This church, which was built by the Dominicans, and which became a parish about 1544, was afterwards raised to a collegiate, but the chapter has ceased to exist since the revenues were reduced to nothing; the title however still remains, and the parish priest is called the *Prior*, as was also the head of the chapter. He receives an annuity of 100 rupees, which is more than the Vicars' allowances; but as he has no casual profits and hardly any occupations, he does not reside near his church, nor even in the city, but only comes thither for the Masses of obligation, or when his duty calls him. The church is shut up constantly, except during Mass.

The church of Our Lady of Light, or *Luz*, is very ancient and situated on the southern hill, which commands the view of the town. It was made a parish at the same time as the preceding, and was likewise raised afterwards to a collegiate. Every thing that has been said concerning the church of the Rosary may be applied to this. The *Prior,* who does not reside in it, receives the same salary of 100 rupees. There are at present but eight communicants. The patronal feast is kept on the 5th of August.

The church of St. Thomas, the Apostle, is in the great street of St. Paul's college, at a furlong distant from it, and on the same side. It was made a parish after the two preceding churches, but never became a collegiate. It is now very poor and in ruins, as well as the adjoining presbytery, or priest's house. The Vicar does not reside in Goa, and Mass is celebrated only on Sundays and Festivals. On St. Thomas's day, the 21st December, the canons of the cathedral and deputations of the convents, come hither in procession, after the High Mass of the cathedral is over, and before that of the church commences, bringing back the reliquary of the Saint, which is carried to the cathedral on the eve of the vespers, by the members of a confraternity attached to this parish. The number of its communicants amount to twenty-four. The Vicar's salary is 75 rupees, like that of all the others in the diocese.

The church of St. Lucia, in the suburb of Lower Dowji, was erected into a parish at the same time as those of Rosary and *Luz*, and it comprehends a small part of the city. The number of communicants now amounts to fifty-six. The Vicar resides in his house adjoining the church, and celebrates Mass every day. The patronal feast is on the 13th of December.

The church of St. Peter, in the suburb of the same name, called also Pannely, though not so ancient as the former, and not much larger, is in a far better state of preservation ; as the number of communicants amounts to one thousand five hundred, some of whom are wealthy for the country, the casual profit is much greater, and goes along with the usual salary, sufficient for the decent maintenance of a priest.

Of the chapel or extra parochial church of the Five Wounds, we have already spoken.

All these churches, as well as the generality of the parish churches in the diocese, and all over the parts of India, now or formerly in possession of the Portuguese, are built nearly on the same plan. A single nave, large or small, with windows much elevated from the ground, a choir about the same size, semi-circular at the end, and communicating with the body of the church by a vault, somewhat smaller than either ; so that, on the two sides or angles of the nave are two altars, and when the edifice is too small, the mere representation of altars ; the main altar is at the extremity of the choir, a large silver or copper lamp, always lighted, hangs down low before it, near the balustrade or railing. The gilding in all these churches about the altars are, or were very rich, and except on festivals they are generally covered with red baize. On solemn occasion, chiefly on the patronal feast, all the walls of the church are hung up and covered with rich silk stuffs of different colours, which present a very fine sight when they are new, but which is not often the case. The poorest of these churches have proofs of their former opulence in their chalices and other vases, which are mostly all of silver, gilt, and of good workmanship. But all the priests' vestments are now no better than old things. At the lower end of the church, over the entrance, is a gallery, chiefly intended for singers, musicians, and for the organs, when there are any, as all the high Masses among the Portuguese, are accompanied with music. Some of these churches have towers, spires, or small domes; but generally, the bells are suspended in apertures, made in the form of windows, in a wall adjoining the front wall on one of the sides of the church; this wall has a platform behind, for the ringers to ascend, and is terminated above by more or less small spires, the highest and middle one of which has a cross over it. The churches that have revenues to afford it, are whitewashed a-new every year, which gives them a very neat appearance.

The Chapels of Goa, and its Suburbs.

Besides the church of *Bom Jesus*, which may be now considered only as a chapel, and of which we shall speak hereafter, the chapels of the city, are those of St. Catherine, of St. Antony of Padua on Mount Rosary, and that of Our Lady of the Mount behind the convent of St. Dominic. The first has no other chaplain but the monks of the neighbouring convent of St. Francis, who perform Masses therein, on certain days in the year, for which the convent receives yearly sixty rupees. The chapel of St. Antony of Padua, has a regular chaplain, who is in the receipt of ninety rupees a year, which is more than what the Vicars receive. That of Our Lady of the Mount has, for chaplain, a canon of the cathedral, who occupies the houses adjoining it, and receives nothing else for his chaplainship. There is a chapel of Our Lady *de Doloribus*, in the suburb of Pannely, before the Archbishop's palace on the causeway. In these chapels, Masses are celebrated only on the patronal feasts, and on certain days for the souls of the founders of those monuments of piety, but never on Sundays.

The Inquisition and Ecclesiastical Courts of Goa.

Of the establishment of the Inquisition of Goa we have already made mention in the preceding paragraph; we have also stated that it took place in 1560; and we have likewise expressed ourselves sufficiently, to shew our true opinion, but entire impartiality, concerning that too famous institution; we will therefore only add here, something relating to the palace, where the inquisition was held, and of its decaying state since the suppression of that institution. The palace of the inquisition faces the new senate house, and lies consequently on the south side of the cathedral square; its front, adorned with three lofty vaults, and ascended by large stone steps, must have been very handsome; it is now raised one story above the ground floor. The breadth is about seventy feet and as to the length, it cannot be ascertained, being surrounded with walls covering about two acres of ground. The reader may consult Dellon, concerning the inside of this building, the distribution, dimensions, and cleanliness of the cells of the prisoners, the police observed within, and the care taken of the captives, &c. At present, the whole is fast decaying: there are no doors nor window cases now existing; shrubs, thorns, and rubbishes choke up the entrance, and the interior must be filled with serpents and other reptiles. It was in 1812, at the time that the British Government had a garrison in Goa, that orders came from the court of Rio Janeiro, at the recommendation of that of London for the suppression of the inquisition. The Inquisitors then four in number, were sent to Portugal, or had leave to remain in Goa, in the enjoyment of their former salaries, during their natural lives. There was not then in the inquisition a single prisoner, and no one living in Goa recollects to have seen any *acto de fe*;

but men of middle age have heard their fathers relate that they had been witnesses to some. So that, there are more than 80 years for certain that such a thing took place, or that any one was executed by the orders of that tribunal.

The members of the ecclesiastical court of Goa, consist of the Archbishop and four priests, secular or regular, but of whom two at least must be the dignitaries or canons of the cathedral. The first is called the *Provisor*, and the second, the *Promotor*; they assemble when and where they are convoked by the Archbishop. Their jurisdiction is exercised chiefly in matrimonial and other ecclesiastical causes, and in admonishing, or punishing the members of the secular clergy; these punishments do not extend beyond a seclusion into one of the seminaries, or some other religious houses; or for greater offences, into the *Aljube*, or prison of the ordinary. The Archbishop, who has alone the power of suspending, or excommunicating, &c., can also order a seclusion, or imprisonment, by his sole power.

The *Aljube* of which Dellon gives a frightful description, is now much altered for the better; it is a neat stone building, with a court towards the *south* of it. The *Provisor* of the ecclesiastical court has the superintendence thereof, and visits it regularly once a month or oftener if necessary. It very seldom contains any prisoners.

The Convents and Religious Orders of Goa.

Franciscans.

The Order of the Franciscans was the first established in Goa, as the members thereof were the chaplains of the first Portuguese vessels that came out to India. It is well known that the Order of St. Francis, soon after the death of its founder, was divided into two distinct congregations, the Conventuals and the Observantines, which latter professed to observe the rules more strictly and with a greater spirit of poverty; these have always been by far the most numerous; and the head of all the Franciscans, who resides at Rome, must be a member of them. The Observantines were those known in France, under the name of *Cordeliers*; in other countries, they are called Franciscans simply, or Franciscans of the Observance. It is to this congregation that all those of Goa, originally belonged. The great convent is close to the cathedral, on the western side; and though inferior to those of the Augustinians and Dominicans, and that of *Bom-Jesus,* it is nevertheless large and well built: some parts however want reparation; the church, on the contrary, is one of the best preserved, best built, and best ornamented in Goa; the vestry is still pretty rich, chiefly, the chalices and other vases. The choir, in which the church-office is sung or recited daily, is in the gallery at the lower end of the church, as in the parish churches, only that there are stalls and a desk as in regular choirs. In general, all the convents of Goa have their choirs placed similarly, except that of St. Dominic; and since only a few years, that of St. Augustine, has a second choir in the usual place, between the altar and the body of the church, and which they use on festivals. The church of St. Francis has two or three very good organs. This convent, before 1600, had several other inferior convents of its Order, of which it was the head or provincial house, both in Goa, and all the other towns of the Portuguese in the East. But, in the beginning of the 17th century, in consequence of some disagreements that took place among the monks of the great convent, and that of the *Mother of God,* in the parish of St. Joseph, or Upper Dowji, the latter house was separated with due authorization, and was annexed to a reformed congregation of Franciscans, called in Italy, Zacolanti, or *Recollects*, and in Spain and Portugal, *Reformed Franciscans of St. Peter of Alcantara.* This house then became the head and provincial convent of that reform in India, as the other convents were divided between the two congregations in proportion to the number of members of each. The convent of the reformed Franciscans, though pretty large, is not nearly so as the great convent; and the church is very small. Both these convents are governed immediately by a superior, called *Guardian*, and constitute the residence of the Fathers Provincials, who, on certain solemn occasions appear at the head of the whole community over the *Guardians*, and who then officiate at all the church offices. He has two *Definitors*, who are his councillors, and two other monks, who have the title of *Visitors*, but who do not exercise that function since several years, which is also the case in all the other convents. The *Guardians*, or local superiors, have likewise supplicants and assistants, and the third charge in the convent, is always that of Master of the Novices. The Franciscans of the Observance, or old Franciscans, at present reckon about thirty members, both professed novices and lay brothers; and they have still an *hospice* and church called *Luz*, near St. Thome or Meliapor, now a suburb of Madras, and some *hospices* and parishes in the diocese of Goa, and the college of St. Bonaventure, at some distance west of the *head* house. This college, which is sufficiently large and has a tolerable though small church, was destined for the young professed members of the Order, to study philosophy, and divinity; but of late the masterships have been transferred to the convents, the college being now only nominal, with two priests and a lay brother, who remain in it to keep it up.

The reformed Franciscans, besides their head convent of *Mater Dei*, have convents at Macao, Daman, and Diu, and that of Cabo, near the western point of the island, (wherein five monks reside) and a college called *De Pilar*, at a small distance south of the city. The number of members of the whole province does not amount to more than twenty-four.

All the Franciscans of India wear the habit of their order, which here consists of a long robe of common cotton cloth, dyed black, with large cowls, which they seldom draw over their heads, and a white girdle, but without scapular. They all shave, and it is improperly that the reformed Franciscans are called by the people of Goa, *Capuchos*, for they are quite different from the Capuchins, which form a distinct reform and congregation of Franciscans, the members of which all wear beards.

The provincial, guardian, and other officers of these two convents and provinces, are re-elected, by the older members of the order, every three years. The provincial is confirmed by the apostolical Nuncio in Portugal, representing the generals of all the religious orders residing at Rome, who, by a special agreement between the King and the Pope, delegate to him all their powers for the monks of their order, all over the Portuguese dominions. The Franciscans of Goa, either ancient or reformed, are very poor, having scarcely sufficient to maintain their convents; they go about begging at stated times, according to the rules of their order.

The Jesuits.

Although the Jesuits have been excluded the Portuguese dominions ever since 1761, they are nevertheless set down here, on account of their being the second order by rank of antiquity in Goa, and the richest, best informed, and most powerful; as well as on account of some of their houses still subsisting.

The Order of the Jesuits is too well known to need saying any thing here concerning it, St. Francis Xavier, one of the first disciples of St. Ignatius, and of the first members of their order, introduced them into Goa, in 1543, in which year they took possession of the college and church of St. Paul, as we have said already. Some years after, they rebuilt the same in the state in which it was, when it was abandoned. Finding, however, the situation unhealthy, they built another college, called St. Rock, on Mount Rosary, close to that church and very near the Augustinian convent. The college of St. Paul then became the noviciate. In 1584, they founded their chief or professed house, to be the residence of the provincial and the oldest and principal members, in the lower part of the city. That house is the one which is still adjoining the church of *Bom-Jesus.* They built this church with great magnificence, and transferred therein the body of St. Francis Xavier; they afterwards acquired the church and college of Chorão, on the island of that name, and those of Rachol in the province of Salsette; they soon abandoned the houses of St. Paul and St. Rock, or kept in them only a few invalid members, (as the Franciscans do now in the college of St Bonaventure) and removed their college to Rachol, and their noviciate to Chorão, as being places more salubrious, or rather less unhealthy than the city. On the suppression of this order, the houses and churches of St. Paul and of St. Rock were suffered to go to ruins; the three other houses were erected into colleges or seminaries.

The house and church of *Bom-Jesus*, were first given to the Italian priests of the congregation of St. Vincent of Paul, called in France, Lazarists; there was then established the chief seminary of the diocese; but about twenty years later, in consequence of some misunderstanding between them and the Portuguese, they were expelled Goa, and all the students removed from Rachol to Chorão. This convent is the largest and finest, after those of St. Augustine and St. Dominic: it is raised two stories above the ground floor. The church, built in the form of a regular cross, is very fine and lofty; it has but three altars, and no gallery, as the Jesuits were not in the habit of singing in the choir. North of the altar, at the extremity of the northern branch of the transept, is the shrine of St. Francis Xavier, which is in copper, beautifully carved and gilt, seated above a lofty and very elegant monument of black marble of Italy. On the four faces are represented, in basso-relievo, the principal actions of the Saint; and on three sides are altars also of marble, and forming a part of the monument. On the third side, the wall is perforated by a large window, or vault over the altar in the inside of the church, which is the chief altar in honour of the Saint. His statue, of solid silver, is exposed over the altar, against the monument, during the *Novena* that precedes his festival, which is celebrated throughout all the Catholic churches on the 3rd of December. During this *Novena* a High Mass is sung every day before the altar and monument of the Saint, and private Masses almost continually said from day-break till nine o'clock, by priests from all parts of the colony, who come thither with a great concourse of people to perform their devotions. On the festival day, the clergy of the cathedral come and sing the whole church office, beginning on the eve with the first vespers. The High

Mass is pontifically celebrated, at the high altar, by the Archbishop, in the presence of the Governor, the members of the administration, the deputations from all the convents and churches of Goa, and an immense crowd of people. The panegyric of the Saint is always preached on this occasion. During the rest of the year, Mass is celebrated every day, but not regularly, or with any obligation thereto. As St. Ignatius is the true patron of this church, his festival is also still solemnized. The church is now under the care of one of the canons of the cathedral, who has the title of *Administrator.* He lives in the house, and performs all the Masses of obligation ; and with his revenues, as canon, he is said to make a sum of nine hundred rupees a year, which is certainly the richest benefice in Goa, without excepting the deanery. The vestry room of this church is vaulted, and it is the finest in Goa, and surpassing many a church itself in beauty. Behind the monument, in a passage leading from the vestry to the convent, is a true picture of St. Francis Xavier, taken shortly after his death, when his body was well preserved. The two houses of Rachol and Chorão, formerly belonging to the Jesuits, having now become the seminaries of the diocese, entrusted to the congregation of St. Philip Neri, we shall speak of them when we shall treat of that order, but advert to them in the mean time in the following paragraph on the subject of education.

The Dominicans.

The Dominicans, or brother preachers, an order instituted by St. Dominic, a Spanish prebendary of the cathedral of Osma, and confirmed by Pope Honorius III. in 1216, has been ever since that time one of the most celebrated orders in Christendom. It produced a great number of Bishops and Cardinals, four Popes, and six Archbishops of Goa. Though the Dominicans came to this city shortly after its conquest, and contributed, chiefly to the foundation of the parochial church of the Rosary, they nevertheless were not united into a body, nor did they establish a regular convent until 1548, wherefore they ranked themselves, in order of antiquity, after the Jesuits. It is well known that this order, after that of the Jesuits and the Benedictines, has produced the greatest number of learned men. The study of divinity, philosophy, and of the learned languages, has always been in a flourishing condition among them ; they are to this day considered as the most learned among the religious of Goa. The two last Bishops, consecrated in Portuguese India, which took place in 1825, were two members of this order, Fr. Paul of St. Thomas Aquinas, Archbishop of Cranganor, who died the following year, and Fr. Thomas de Noronha, Bishop of Cochin, lately transferred to Fernambuca in Brasils. They were however, since that year, very much reduced in number, not exceeding twenty-five at Goa, and about ten at Macao, Diu and Mosambique. Among these is now but a single European, who is the administrator or governor of the Bishopric of Cochin. Their convent, situated in the eastern part of the town, is very large and very stately built. The cloisters are magnificent ; the church is rather old and not vaulted, and some parts begin to want reparations. It is spacious, but rather too narrow for its length ; the exterior front, is the finest in Goa. and exceeds, in that respect, even that of St. Augustine, though the latter is much superior in regard to every thing else. The steps, ascending to the church, make a most grand appearance. The college of St. Thomas Aquinas, in the suburb of St. Peter, is likewise spacious, but not so much so as the convent. It is however in a much more healthy situation, whence, many of the elder members of the order, retired from office, and exempted from the duty of daily assisting at the choir, prefer this residence. Besides the young professed members, who are instructed in this college, Seculars are also admitted to the lectures; this college on the water side, was founded about the beginning of the 17th century. The Dominicans have likewise the church and house of St. Barbara, between Ribandar and Pangi, where three monks generally live, and whither the others repair occasionally, for festivals, or change of air. The Dominicans had houses in Cochin, in Meliapor, in Daman, in Diu, in Macao, and in Mosambique; but they have abandoned them all, except in the three last. They still have a handsome church and some houses, paying rent to the order in Meliapor or St. Thome, near Madras; they were formerly very rich, but are not so now, particularly since about twenty years, when a provincial of theirs, shamefully squandered away the revenues and riches of the convent. Nevertheless, they are still supposed to be in the easiest condition, after the Augustinians and the priests of St. Philip of Neri. Their habit is entirely white, consisting of a long robe with a cowl, a girdle and scapular; (which latter is black for the lay-brothers) but when they go out on solemn occasions, and visit persons of dignity, they wear over their habits a black cloak, whence, they were called anciently in England black friars, in opposition to the Carmelites, whose cloak is of the same form, but white, and for which reason they were called white friars. The Dominicans of Portuguese India formed, until lately, a branch of the province of Portugal, governed by a Vicar-general; but now it forms a distinct province. The Superior, however, continues to take the same title, though he has a right to be entitled Provincial; the local Superior of every houses, as is well known, is called *Prior* ; and all are elected every three years, by the members having the right of voting.

The Augustinians.

The Augustinians were the fourth religious order established in Goa. They owe their origin to St. Augustine himself, who established a society of priests, with whom he lived in common, first at Tagasta in Africa, his native country, before he became Bishop, and afterwards at Hypona, when he was consecrated for that See. The successors of his first disciples led an hermitical life till the 12th century, when Pope Innocent IV. in 1248, authorised them to live in the cities and towns, and render themselves useful by preaching to and instructing the people, as the Dominicans, Franciscans, and Carmelites, which were then called the mendicant orders, from their subsisting chiefly by begging alms of the faithful. This custom is only kept up for the form in most Catholic countries, except amongst the strictest branches of the Franciscans. The others were permitted to have revenues in common, or to receive stipulated alms, given at regular times, by charitable persons. It is well known that Martin Luther was a member of this order, and as his defection rendered the Augustinians odious in several Catholic countries, they obtained from the Pope leave of changing the colour of their usual habit, from black to white, which is exactly like that of the Dominicans, except, that they wear a black leather girdle, and never make use of a cloak, or overall. But on great festivals, both in the choir and in public processions, and on all visits, or occasions of ceremony, they resume their ancient black habit, which is exactly of the same form as the white. The Augustinians came to Goa in 1572, being twelve in number, under

Fr. Antonio *de Paixão,* who was their first provincial. In the same year, they laid the foundation of their convent, in the place where it now stands, on the mountain of the Rosary, but on a much inferior scale. It was shortly after extended and rebuilt in its present state, and dedicated under the title of the convent of Grace (*de Graça*), on the 9th of September, 1597. It is certainly a most beautiful and stately convent or building of Goa. Few cities in Europe can boast of a finer edifice of the kind ; the cloisters, pillars, galleries, halls, and cells, are all most beautiful, the church forming the northern side thereof and facing the west, with the choir towards the east, like ancient churches ; it is remarkable for the loftiness and boldness of its great vault, but the side aisles are indeed rather narrow in comparison. There are eleven altars all well and richly ornamented, chiefly the high altar ; a choir for festival days with stalls has been made lately, at the foot of the steps leading up to the sanctuary or altar area, as in the cathedral, Dominican, and conventual churches in general, and as in the other parts of the world ; but on ordinary and daily occasions, the choir of the gallery is used, according to the custom of all the convents in Goa. This convent, both from its revenues and its situation, which is the healthiest in Goa, is now the best provided in the diocese. Sons of the best families in the country, who wish to devote themselves to the Church, enter this convent by preference ; there are more European members in this order, than in any others.* They reckon in all near fifty members, besides three or four at Macao, and from twelve to fifteen in Bengal and other parts of India. The Mission of Bengal is the chief source of their opulent situation ; the two Catholic churches of

* At present there are four or five European Augustinians, either in Goa, or in Bengal. The Provincial is one of them.

Calcutta, one of which is the richest now in all India, and all the other churches in Bengal, under the British dominions, are exclusively entrusted to the care of the members of this order, sent directly from Goa, though they take the faculties, or licenses, of exercising the ministry, from the Bishop, or administrator of St. Thomè, or Meliapor, near Madras, who is commonly, since near a century, a member of the same order. Besides the Missions of Bengal, and the great convent of Goa, they have the adjoining college, called *De Populo,* for the instruction of the younger members of their order, founded in 1602: (a very fine building, joined to the convent by an arch over the street, with a decent and sufficiently large church) the noviciate, which is contiguous on the north of the convent, and which may be considered as a part thereof, a country house in the interior of the island, a large and well-preserved convent in Daman, with a country house and other revenues, a small hospice lately established at Bombay, for the travelling members of the order, another at St. Thomè, or Meliapore, near Madras, and the convent of Macao. The convent at Diu is abandoned and in ruins for want of revenues. Although this be the richest and most numerous order of Goa, it never formed a particular province, but a congregation, or branch of the province of Portugal; nevertheless, the chief in India has always been dignified with the title of *Provincial* to this very day. The present chief is the hundred and seventeenth since the commencement of the establishment; he is elected every three years. The election was formerly made simply by the voting members of the Indian province, as in the other convents of Goa; but on account of some disturbances, that took place since some sixty years ago, another mode was adopted; the voting members all give their votes in sealed letters for the election of the future Provincial, the dignitors, visitors, the prior of Goa, the rector of the college, and the other principal members. The existing Provincial sends them all to Lisbon, where, the Provincial of Portugal, along with the chief members of the province, open the letters, and according to the most numerous votes therein contained, they design the persons to be elected; taking care, that for every office, three individuals be named; the first of whom is to enter into office immediately; but in case of his death or refusal, the second; and in case of the death or refusal of the second, the third fills the vacant place. These elections, or nominations, are all sealed and sent back to Goa, and the *Provincial* opens them in the presence of the whole community, and immediately the newly elected enter into office. As to the heads of the smaller convents, and members of inferior offices, they are provided for by a simple and ordinary election in Goa.

The Carmelites.

The barefooted Carmelites, were a reform of Carmelites, instituted in Spain, in the 16th century, by St. Theresa and St. John *De Cruz*, which soon spread over all Catholic Europe. The Order of the Carmelites pretend to be the oldest in Christendom, or even older than Christianity itself; since they look upon the prophets Elias and Eliseus, as their first founders, who established them on Mount Carmel. They believe, they had successors until the coming of Christ, and that certain members of them were at Jerusalem on the day of Pentecost, when the Holy Ghost descended upon the Apostles; that at the wonderful miracle of the Apostles being heard at once to speak in all the languages in use, among the multitude present at the festival, they were of the number of the three thousand converts, who were the fruit of St. Peter's first sermon; that having put themselves under the special protection of the Blessed Virgin Mary, then living, they went back to their convent on Mount Carmel; and that upon their report, all the Order declared themselves disciples of Christ. Whether this be true or not, it is certain they existed in the same place at the time of the crusades, and that, one of the Latin Patriarchs of Jerusalem, gave them a convent in that city, got them confirmed by the Pope, and had them established in Rome, much about the same time as the Augustinians. The Pope ordered them to observe the rule of St. Augustine with some modifications, as the Dominicans and several other new orders had done, and they were ranked among the mendicant orders. Their dress is similar, in form, to that of the Dominicans, but the colour of their usual habit is dark purple, and the cloak or overall, which they wear when they go out on solemn occasions, is white. There never was but one reform of this order, which we have mentioned; and its members differ only from the non-reformed, by wearing sandals, and no shoes or stockings besides observing the rule more rigorously. The barefooted Carmelites established Missions in Bagdad and in Persia, early in the beginning of the 16th century; and in 1607, they established a convent at Goa; since which they got the Missions of Surat, of the Catholic Syrians of Malabar, of Bombay, and of the interior or western part of the Mogul empire. But the island of Salsette, near Bombay, and the town and territory of Basseen, having been taken by the Mahrattas; and the British masters of Bombay, having thought proper to take the Catholic parishes of the island from the Franciscans of Goa, and to entrust them to the care of the Carmelites of Surat, the authorities of Goa, were greatly exasperated against the latter, and expelled them from the Portuguese dominions, and gave their church and convent to the priests of St. Philip of Neri, newly established in Goa, who made it their college, which continues to be so still; the convent and church situated between the ancient college of St. Paul, and the convent of the Dominicans, on a hill, are still in good repair, and are well-built edifices, though much inferior to the others of the same kind, which we have mentioned. The late Archbishop of Goa, being of the order, would have willingly re-established it with Portuguese members from Europe, but, not being able to accomplish this design, he instituted a community of secular priests, bound only by simple vows to observe the rule of the barefooted Carmelites, and to wear the habit of the order; he built them a convent between Ribandar and Pangi, near the Dominican house of St. Barbara, which the people call the convent of *Chimbel.* As the Theatins and priests of St. Philip de Neri, as we shall say presently, were then all of the Brahminical caste, and received only such in their communities, the new institution was composed exclusively of *Chardos*, which is the second caste, and who pretend to be genuine Khatrias, as we are going to mention. This convent is the poorest in the colony, and contains about sixteen monks.

The Theatins or Order of St. Cajetan.

The Theatins were instituted in Italy, about the same time as the Jesuits, by St. Cajetan of Thienna, and by John Caraffa, who became afterwards Pope, under the name of Paul IV.; but who being then Archbishop of *Theato* or *Chieti*, in the kingdom of Naples, the name of that city was given to the new institution. This order call themselves, *the regular Clerks of Divine Providence*, because the chief thing required by their rules is to possess no revenue whatever, and yet not to beg, but to trust entirely, for subsistence, to the beneficial kindness of Providence, and to the spontaneous charities of the faithful ; they make solemn vows, but live rather like secular priests, and like the Jesuits, than like monks, being occupied with preaching the word of God to the faithful, and administering the sacraments, leading the rest of the time a very regular and retired life ; their habit is that of the secular clergy, with some very slight difference; but they wear a long rosary hanging from their neck. They were established in Goa, in the middle of the 17th century, near the Viceroy's palace, by members, sent from Italy ; and they built a small, but most beautful church, all arched, with a fine dome or *capola,* after the model of that of St. Peter's at Rome. The Italian founders were soon joined by many of the natives, and since more than fifty years, there have been no Europeans among them, and they receive only members of the Brahminical class. They are very poor and have no other considerable place of abode ; but they are now intrusted with the mission of Masulipatam, and likewise with that of the French settlement of Yanaom. They correspond directly with their general in Italy, through the channel of the Nuncio at Lisbon ; and their Superior in India, elected every three years has the title of *Prefect.* These religious men are the most esteemed, and held in the greatest veneration in Goa ; they are the usual confessors of the greatest part of the laity, but few enter this order, on account of its poverty, of the exclusion given to all but Brahmins, and of the unwholesome air of the convent, which is the worst in the city. Few of them ever enjoy their health a long time, and the greatest part of them are always sick ; there are but about fifteen members of this order in India. Besides the stateliness of the church, the gilding and decorations of the chief altar, which are truly admirable, the convent and cloisters are small, and have nothing worthy of remark.

Order of St. John of God.

This is an order of lay-brothers, for the taking care of the sick in the hospitals, instituted in Spain in the 17th century by a holy man, named *John*, and surnamed, of *God*, because, he repeated constantly that name; they came to Goa about the 17th century, and their convent or chief housé, in front of St. Augustine on Mount Rosary, is small as well as the church; there is only one or two priests among them, to act as chaplains; there are now about twelve members only of this order in Goa, who are natives, and, mostly, of a very dark complexion; six reside in the Royal hospital of *Polvora*, in Pannely, the rest in the convent; they have hospitals in Daman, Diu, Macao, &c., but for want of subjects, many of those houses are now kept by seculars.

THE CONGREGATION OF THE PRIESTS OF ST. PHILIP OF NERI.

St. Philip of Neri established this congregation in Rome, at the same time that St. Ignatius instituted the order of the Jesuits; they were called Oratorians, and soon spread through Italy, France, Spain, Portugal, &c. They are secular priests, who make only simple vows, and live in common, occupying themselves in preaching, but still more, in the instruction of youth. It is well known how many colleges they had in France at the time of the revolution. Though established the last of all the orders in Goa, they form now the most numerous and richest, after that of St. Augustine; but they are all exclusively Brahmins, like the Theatins, and wear the same dress; the church of the Miraculous Cross, on the mountain adjoining Luz, on the south of the city, which had belonged originally to the Augustians, was given to them; and adjoining to it, they built their chief house, which is very large, and looks the newest building in the whole city; its situation is remarkably healthy for the country; they have no cloisters in their convent, nor choirs in the churches, like the monks; because they recite their office privately, like the secular clergy, and go only to church for Mass, morning and evening prayers, meditations, and other devotions, which they perform in common. We have already said, that the ancient convent of the Carmelites has been given to them for their college, where the young members of their community are instructed; the two ancient colleges of Chorão and Rachol, which are now the two Archiepiscopal seminaries, are intrusted to their care. The seminary of Chorão, opposite the suburb of St. Peter, in the island of which it bears the name, is a large and fine building with a good church on a hill. Behind the house is a small chapel, with an elegant dome, and Grecian pillars supporting the edifice; giving the whole from a distance, the true appearance of a scenery of Greece. This place, is, however, now become extremely unhealthy, so that the number of boarders and out-students is much inferior to that of Rachol, which is likewise a very fine building, in the parish of that name, in the province or peninsula of Salsette, and only about a day's journey from Goa by water; in both houses are settlements for a superior, a professor of divinity, one of philosophy, and one of grammar, who are all members of the congregation, and for three singers or chorists, and twelve students; others are admitted as boarders, at 7 rupees a month, or as day scholars; and not only those youths who are destined for the church, but seculars, otherwise engaged, are also admitted; the boarders are obliged to wear the clerical dress, and the out-scholars the secular, unless they received the tonsure. The chief source of the funds of this congregation, is the Catholic mission of Ceylon, amounting to about 100,000 souls, with whose spiritual direction they are exclusively charged, though, they are obliged to take their faculties from the Bishop, or administrator of Cochin. There are about twelve priests employed in that mission, and the number of those residing in the three houses of Goa, amount to near fifty.

General Observations Regarding the Friars or Relioious Order of People in Goa.

By all that has been already said concerning each order established in Goa, it must be concluded that, there are about two hundred Friars, or religious order of people, all of whom, except the priests of the congregation of St. Philip Neri, the Carmelites of the convent of *Chimbel*, and the novices of all the orders, are bound by the tripple and solemn vows of chastity, poverty, and obedience; this obedience consists in being submissive in all things to their superior, chiefly with respect to their residence; so that, when sent afar off from their community, for any function whatever, even when living alone, they cannot stir more than twenty miles from the place designed for their residence, or the place allotted to their mission, without a special leave from their superiors, under pain of being considered as apostates; they observe the vow of poverty, by possessing nothing but in common. However, since the convents have become poor, they are permitted to receive alms for Masses, sermons, &c., and to gain some trifling sums, by means proper to clergymen, in order to ameliorate the scanty pittance, which the convent allows them; they are permitted also to receive some pecuniary relief from their families and friends, and the little, they thus acquire, they may dispose of as they please at their death, by special license from Rome. This is, however, a deviation from the general use in Catholic countries, in which the professed religious are not permitted to make wills, wherefore, the strictest among them do not avail themselves of this license. As to the vow of chastity, it is a formal and solemn vow, which they make long before they enter in holy-orders, when they incur the obligation at the same time of reciting the daily church office, either in common, or privately, like the secular clergymen. The difference between the two, respecting chastity is this: that the religious makes a formal vow of it, whilst the secular clergyman, merely receives an order, to which he knows, that the obligation of leading a simple and holy life, until his death, is attached as an indispensable condition; the professed lay-brothers, among the religious, enter into the same vows as the choristers, who aspire to holy-orders; but then they are not obliged to recite the church office, but only to assist at some part of it in the choir, on certain days, or occasions; their business being to do, or superintend, all the temporal business and daily service of the house. In Goa, the lay-brothers are few, not more than three or four in each convent; every member of the community who has exercised one of the superior functions, or who is of five years' profession, is allowed a servant, whom he pays, but who is fed by the house; there are also servants attached to the convent, in general, for all the grosser works; the church office is sung, or recited, every day in the choir, and a solemn conventual Mass always said; but the members in high functions, or who have exercised them, are all exempted from attendance, except on solemn days, and on those, in which it is their duty to officiate, having each their week, or festivals, appointed them; they are likewise dipensed from assisting, except on days of ceremonies, at the canon table, with the young professed and novices; they have leave to go out on their private concerns, whilst the others must have the permission of the *Prior*, or Superior of the house, to do so; they are allowed two meals a day, besides a slight breakfast. At dinner, they receive a portion of flesh-meat, except on days of abstinence; the rest of the meal, and the supper, consist entirely of fish, rice, and vegetables; those, who eat privately, in their cells, can add whatever more they can procure themselves. On the patronal feast of each convent, that is, of the founders of their order, as on the festivals of St. Augustine, St. Dominic, St. Francis, &c., they celebrate their office with very great pomp and solemnity; the Governor, or Viceroy, several magistrates, and members of other convents, or of the secular order, assist thereat, and partake of a suitable repast, after the morning service. The Archbishop and the other Provincials are never invited, because it is the privilege of the provincial of the house to officiate on that day, which would be a kind of incivility in the presence of the others, and more so of the Archbishop; but the prelate comes and officiates pontifically at the vespers, or evening office, and gives the Benediction of the Blessed Sacrament. These festivals are called in Goa, the *Patriarchal Festivals*. The young professed members, begin the study of the Latin language, immediately after entering into their vows, and remain in the convent. When they are sufficiently instructed for the study of philosophy and divinity, they go to the college of the order, and being duly prepared, they are presented by the provincial to the Archbishop for holy-orders; the Archbishop has them examined first, and if he is not satisfied, or finds any other objection, he can refuse admitting them. This is the chief exercise of his authority over the convents, and as for the rest, he can only authorise them to hear confessions out of their order, and can prohibit their saying Mass elsewhere, when he has his reasons for so doing; with regard to all other points, they are entirely under the jurisdiction and the direction of their *Prior*, or local Superior. They have some vacations throughout the year, generally, of a fortnight each, during which, they may go and reside with their families or friends.

The morals of the monks, chiefly of Spain and Portugal, have been severely censured since a long time, but, with what justice, I do not pretend to determine; nor can I undertake to assert, that there has been any change or amelioration in that point, as I have never been in those countries. The regular clergy of Goa, participated in that general accusation; but though I cannot tell what may have been the case about a hundred years ago, yet, I can venture to affirm, that it would be the greatest injustice, and a horrid calumny, to pretend, that the actual Friars, or Religious of Goa, are in the least deserving of such a censure at present. It is a certain fact, regarding which I will speak again in the next paragraph, that there has been an utter change for the better, in the manners and morals of the Indo-Portuguese, for since more than a century. The clergy and monks, far from being an exception, to this laudable change, afford, in general, the example of the most regular and clerical life. The monks, indeed, are yet taxed with being less strict, and, except some Augustinians, Dominicans, and members of the congregation of St. Philip, are, in general, less instructed in Latin, Philosophy, and Divinity, than the secular priests; but they must be allowed this advantage over the latter, that they are much more liberal minded, have less country and local prejudices, are much more polished in their manners, and, upon the whole, much more amiable members of society. It is to be observed, that the cloister law is strictly attended to, that is, that no women whatever, under pain of excommunication, can pass the threshold of any convent of men; they are only allowed to go into the body of the church by the great door.

I have thought that the details, in which I have entered here, respecting the divers orders of Goa, individually and generally, might afford a gratification to the curiosity of an English reader, in whose native country all those orders are now unknown; and therefore the little I have said, concerning the origin of each order, will serve them as an introduction to the knowledge of the present state of a numerous part of the Catholic Indian clergy, regarding whom, I am sorry to say, very erroneous and unjust notions are entertained. I have deemed it an act of strict justice, to exculpate them from accusations, which they by no means deserve; though some of their predecessors, or brothers, in Europe, may have given some occasion to their being made formerly.

THE NUNNERY OR MONASTERY OF ST. MONICA.

This house was founded by the celebrated Don Fr. Alexo de Menezes, Archbishop of Goa, who gave it the rule of St. Augustine, to whose order he belonged, and dedicated it to the holy Mother of that celebrated Doctor; this is the only Nunnery in Goa. There are in it commonly thirty nuns, comprehending the novices, among whom are still some European females, but the generality are natives; they make the same vows as the monks, and can never stir out of the house, from the day of their profession to their death; the convent is on the north side of St. Augustine's square, and the ground thereof occupies a part of the hill sloping down back of it; the cloisters are said to be very fine, and the chapel on the square, open to the public, is small, and has but one altar; the nuns have their choir in the gallery, like the monks, but a veil, through which they may see the priest at the altar without being seen themselves, hides them from public view. They recite the church office daily, and answer the priest at High Mass; below, near the altar, is a gate, through which they confess and receive communion; no man, but the doctor, and some old black slaves, are acting as gardeners; and a priest to administer extreme unction to a dying nun, is allowed to step within the cloister. Even secular women, except servants or boarders, are not habitually admitted; if any one wishes to speak to a nun, she is called to the door by the porters, and commonly another nun accompanies her; every year, however, the Archbishop, to whom this convent is immediately subject, according to the institution of the founder, performs his visitation in the interior, in company with his grand vicar and another priest; the usual chaplain, the confessor, and the steward, are monks of the neighbouring Augustine convent, appointed by the Provincial; the nuns wear a white dress; they elect the Prioress and her assistants every three years, and afterwards obtain the confirmation of the Archbishop; the number of female servants in this house is very great; the nuns make scapularies, *Agnus Dei,* chain beads, and rosaries, &c.; they also make excellent fruit preserves and syrups, which are all sold for the benefit of the house; it is besides pretty richly endowed, and the nuns lead a very holy life, and are much esteemed in the colony.

CASAS DE MISERICORDIA.

The confraternity, or brotherhood of *Misercordia,* was formed soon after the conquest, according to the custom of the Portuguese, who established it in every large town of their colonies. It is a mere association of Laymen, for performing good works, as all other charitable societies throughout the Christain world. Archbishop Menezes, about the beginning of the 17th century, determined them to lay out their funds to build three houses, or hospices, one for men, one for widows, and one for virgins ; they all live in community, and have each their superior, but they can quit the establishment when they please ; the virgins, when suitable offers are made, are married, and receive a settlement from the funds of the house ; there are now about thirty-six of them, and the two other houses are filled only with tew most wretched persons, as the unhealthiness of the city prevents any one, but those who cannot absolutely maintain themselves, from accepting a place in these hospices ; each house has a decent chapel, and a chaplain ; in that of the men is a statue of Albuquerque the Great, who first encouraged the association.

PANGI, AND THE NEIGHBOURING VILLAGES.

Pangi, the residence of the Viceroy, or Governor, ever since the administration of Emanuel Saldanha de Albuquerque, Count of Ega, who governed Portuguese India, from 1758 to 1765, as we have said, is now a very handsome town, about three miles west of Goa ; all the houses, well-built, and having generally one story above the ground floor, are always kept white and clean, and have the doors and window frames painted green, and several of them have balconies; the streets are pretty broad, and some are paved; the Viceroy's palace is close to the water, and it is no higher than the other houses, and has not much external appearance; but it is large and has very fine rooms in the inside, both for the lodging of the Governor, and for the different public offices; the other public builings, are a large and fine church, with good revenues,* the custom-house, barracks, and a gaol; the number of communicants in the parish amounts to 2,000, and the number of strangers including Pagans and Mahometans, is supposed to be 6,000; so that the whole population may amount to about 9,000, besides the troops.

The village of Ribandar is between Pangi and Pannely. It is much inferior to either, but has still several good houses and a large church; it is in this village that the chief civil and criminal court or tribunal of the colony is established, and which has, under its immediate jurisdiction, the whole island of Goa, and the other neighbouring islands; it receives appeals from the the two other tribunals of Salsette and Bardes.

The village of St. Agnes, west of Pangi, is trifling. It is only remarkable for its Archiepiscopal palace, which we have already mentioned, and the artillery quarters and barracks.

OF THE ISLAND OF GOA OR TISSUARY IN GENERAL.

The island of Goa, called also *Tissuary*, from its containing originally thirty colleges, is, on an average, about six miles in length, and four in breadth, and lies towards the sea. It terminates, as we have said, by the point of Cabo, near which is a fort, (which serves commonly as a State prison), and a tolerable good convent of reformed Franciscans, very apparent from the sea, being, like the fort on the top of a hill, whence there is a beautiful prospect of the water and country; towards the east, the island is separated by a narrow channel from the mainland, but is fortified by the great wall, of which we have already spoken several

* The Vicars of Pangi, Margão, and Mapuça, are supposed to make a total amount of 1,500 pardaos.

times; the centre of the island is pretty elevated, and the largest plain is towards the east and south east; the climate of this island is far less healthy than that of the provinces of Bardes and Salsette; the chief objects of culture are wheat, pulse, and fruits, chiefly mangoes, but the principal revenues consist in cocoanuts; there are pretty good pastures, and several marshes and ponds of stagnant waters; the number of parishes, besides those of the city and suburbs, now amount to twenty-four; their names are, Pangi, Merces, Ribandar, St. Cross, St. Agnes, Taligao, Bambolim, Seridrao, Nazareth, Curca, Old Goa or St. Andrews, Batim, St. Lawrence, Neura, Mandur, Moula, St. Anna, Asocim, Carambolim, St. Simon's, Corlim, St. Yago or St. James, St. Blasius, and St. Joseph or Upper Dowji. All these parishes are very poor, and are very thinly inhabited; and the churches, for the most part, are small and ruinous, and the vicars have scarcely wherewith to subsist. Excepting Pangi and Goa, with its suburbs, it is calculated that in each parish there may be fifty communicants, on an average, which will make

for twenty-three parishes	1,150
Children, Strangers, Pagans, and Mahometans about one-third more...	383
Pangi, (as said above)	9,000
The City of Goa and its Suburbs (as calculated above)	3,143
Total number in the island	13,676;

so that, the whole island of Goa, according to this computation, cannot contain above 14,000 inhabitants of all ages, sexes, and religions, besides the troops; this number is very small, compared to its ancient population, and, except in Pangi, Ribandar, and Pannely, it continues to diminish every day, as the poverty of the individuals and the unhealthiness of the air, compel yearly a part of them to remove in the province on the mainland, or to emigrate to other parts of India.

THE ISLAND OF CHORAO.

The island, opposite to Ribandar, extends from north to south, and is about three miles long, and less than one broad ; it was formerly pretty populous, but is now almost deserted, being deemed very unhealthy. It is divided into two parishes, that of St. Bartholomew's on the north, and that of Grace on the south ; in the latter of which is the seminary, of which we have spoken several times ; the whole number of individuals on the island is about one hundred and fifty.

THE ISLAND OF DIVAR.

The island, which lies on the S. E. of the preceding, and opposite to the city of Goa, is two miles and a half long, from north to south, and one broad. It is divided into three parishes, Naroa, on the north, St. Mathias, in the centre, and Piedade, on the south. It contains about two hundred and twenty inhabitants.

THE ISLAND OF JUA.

This is a small island on the N. E. of Divar, forming a single parish; it is about three miles in circumference, and may contain seventy or eighty inhabitants.

THE ISLAND OF COMBARJUA.

This island is about the size of the former, and lies on the S. of it, between the new province of Ponda, on the mainland, east, and the island of Goa, west. It forms a part of the parish of St. Blasius, and there are some few other islands near the preceding ones, mostly deserted ; and their population is included in their respective parishes.

THE PROVINCE OF SALSETTE.

This province, or peninsula, is situated on the S. and S. E. end of the island of Goa. It is about twenty miles from east to west, and six miles from north to south; its north-western point is called Murmugao, and gives name to the southern harbour of Goa, which is the safest during the monsoon. The province of Salsette was converted to Christianity, and entirely subjected to the Portuguese, about fifty years after the conquest of Goa. It is now reckoned the best, the most fertile, the most populous, and the most healthy part of the colony; it may contain about 200,000 inhabitants,* almost all Christians, there being very few Hindoos or Mahomedans in this part. It is divided into twenty-eight parishes, but several of them have dependant churches, or chapels of ease, for the neighbouring villages that do not form a parish: the whole amounting to forty-six villages, besides the town of Margão, the capital of the province; their names are, Rachol, Ambora, Raia, Lotulim, Rassaim, Verna, Calata, Quelocim, Nagoa, Cortalim, Sancoale, Daboli, Varim, Chicalim, Murmugao, Pole, Cola, Betalbatim, Velcão, Arossim, Cançaulim, Majorda, Carmona, Cavelossim, Spernabat, Varca, Benaulim, Seraulim, Danaulim, Chinchinim, Sarsora, Paroda, Navelim, Chandor, Guirdolim, and Courtorim.

Margão, the chief town of this province, is situated near the head of a river, running westwardly into the sea. It is nearer the southern and eastern extremities of the peninsula, and though in a central position, the

* The whole Colony is reckoned to contain 380,000 Christians; we have seen that the island of Goa, and the neighbouring islands, do not contain more than 15,000; and allowing as many for the new provinces, there will remain 250,000 for Salsette and Bardes; the latter is somewhat smaller, and has a greater number of Hindoos and Musulmen, so that, by allowing 200,000 inhabitants to Salsette, we shall not deviate much from the truth.

distance from the city is fifteen miles S. S. E. It is well built, and is the largest and most populous town in the colony, and the residence of the most wealthy and respectable inhabitants. It has a large rich church, and a great number of clergymen attached to it, besides the Vicar. It has also a senate house, and a house for the provincial court; and the parish reckoning 6,000 communicants, the entire population, including some few Hindoos and Mahometans, cannot fall much short of 10,000.

Rachol was the chief town, at the time of the conquest by the Portuguese, and the first missions of the Jesuits. It was then a fortress, and the church was, a long time, considered as the first in dignity in Salsette, but is now superceded by that of Margão. The fortifications exist no more, and the town or village, is now only remarkable for being the seat of the first Archiepiscopal seminary, containing generally above sixty students, including those entertained on the public funds, as we have already said. Rachol is, however, not so healthy as Margao. It is about four miles N. E. thereof, on a river opposite to the new province of Ponda, a little more than ten miles S. E. of Goa.

THE PROVINCE OF BARDES.

Bardes extends from N. to S. along the sea coast, north-west of the island of Goa, and is joined to the mainland, by a narrow neck between two rivers, on the N. E. It is not above ten miles from N. to S., and five from E. to W. It however comprises six villages, with their territories beyond the said isthmus, contiguous to the new province of Bicholim. It is not so fertile, nor so healthy, as Salsette, but much more so, than the island of Goa; the S. W. point, forming the northern entrance of the harbour of Goa, is called Aguada, and has a fort and village of that name, with the parochial church of St. Laurence, very conspicuous over the hill, whence, you have a very fine view of the fort of Cabo, of the neighbouring monastery, on the island of Goa. of Marmugao, and part of Salsette, and of the desert islands of St. George, out at sea. Bardes was converted to Christianity shortly after Salsette; there are, however, now in it a great number of Pagans, and some Mahometans, perhaps about 10,000; but the greater part of whom, have come thither of late; the whole population may amount to 160,000. It is divided into twenty-six parishes, and contains thirty-six villages, besides Mapuça, the chief town; their names are, Moura, Ucaçaim, Aldona, Nachinola, Pomburpa, Socorro, Sirula, Penha de Franca, Reis, Nelur, Aguada, Pilerne, Candolim, Saligao, Sangolda, Calangute, Caneca, Nagao, Guirim, Parra, Verula, Baga, Assagaon, Cunchelim, Oxela, Chapora, Seolim, Vagalim, Comorlim, Caluale, Revorra, Naḍora, Pirna, Asnora, Tivim, and Casua; these six last are beyond the isthmus, where was constructed, formerly, a wall, reaching N. and S. from river to river, but which is now almost all in ruins.

Mapuça, the chief town, is situated near a stream, which empties itself into the river that runs from N. to S., separates Bardes from Bicholim and Sanquelim, and falls into the harbour of Goa, forming the island of Chorão. This town is nearer the southern and eastern extremity of the peninsula, and about ten or eleven miles from the city. It is smaller than Margão, but larger than Pangi. It is clean, well-built, and has the usual public buildings, church, senate-house, tribunal or court-house, &c. It reckons 4,000 communicants, and about 9,000 inhabitants of all sexes, ages, and religions.

The Seven new Provinces of the Government of Goa.

These new provinces were acquired to the crown of Portugal since the middle of the eighteenth century: they are, *Pernem*, north of Bardes, *Bicholim*, east of the same, *Sanquelim*, south-east of the preceding, *Urgaon*, south of Sanquelim, *Ponda*, east of the island of Goa, *Zaumbolim*, south-east of Salsette, and *Canacona*, south of the same, and on the sea, extending south to the British territory of Carwar.

It is not easy to determine the extent of these provinces, or the number of the villages they contain, as they are intermixed with those of petty Rajahs, or of the British territory; all these provinces, however, take their name from their chief town or village, which certainly belongs to the Portuguese. The whole number of Portuguese subjects in these provinces, are supposed to amount to somewhat above 100,000, including about 100,000 Christians, divided into four different missions, but not regular parishes, of which there are only four established: namely, Bicholim, Congivan, in the same province, Sanquelim, and Ponda; the latter is an important fortress, at the entrance of a passage through the Ghauts, of which mention has been made several times in the preceding pages.

S. V.—*State of the Population—Government—Religion—Public Instruction—Riches—Revenues—Agriculture—Commerce, and manners of the Inhabitants of the Colony of Goa, at the present time.*

POPULATION.

As we have partially stated above, in describing the different parts of the Colony, the whole Christian population under the Portuguese sway, and under the immediate dependance of the Governor of Goa, is reckoned to amount to 380,000, and the Pagan and Mahometans to about 100,000, making a total of 480,000 ; which, with the transient population, the small, but still kept up, introduction of slaves from Mosambique, and the new acquisition of *Aldeas* in the new provinces, may make in all half a million of souls.

DISTINCTION OF CLASSES OR CASTES.

Although the Indians of Goa, in embracing Christianity, have not retained, like those of the Jesuit and Pondicherry Missions, all those distinctions of castes and ancient usages of Paganism, which have been considered indifferent to religion, they nevertheless keep up that distinction only in respect to marriages, which are most generally, though not always, contracted between members of the same castes ; these castes may therefore be now considered as the different tribes into which the ancient Israelites were divided.

The first class or caste is that of the Europeans, or their children, born in the country, without the probable intention of remaining in it. This class is very small, and confined to the Viceroy, or Governor, and some of his Subalterns, as well as some officers of the army, a few seamen, the Archbishop, and a very few clergymen and monks, and lastly a few soldiers, who marry in the country, and whose children are immediately numbered in the second or mixed class.

The second class is that called the *mistiss*, or mixed class, very much similar to that called among the English, Indo-Britons, though it has a more extensive comprehension, than that term; for it includes even natives of pure European blood, but established in the country since the first generation; these families, although considered in Portugal on the same level with Europeans, and though all *Fidalgos*, or noble men, according to the use introduced into Portuguese India from the origin, are nevertheless comprehended by the Goanese into the mixed race, because, as they say: "*If there is no mixture of blood, there is a mixture of air;*" these families, all very respectable, are not numerous. After these, come all those who are of the mixed European and Indian blood, and who are much more numerous and the greater part poor. The second class, however is still the smallest after the pure Europeans; those descended only from European parents, though after several generations, differ very little in complexion from the Portuguese of Europe; the others have a lighter or deeper shade, according to the proportion of Indian blood they have in them.

The third class or caste, is that of the Brahmins; they are held in high esteem and consideration, though excluded from the greatest privileges of the Europeans and their descendants, which consists chiefly in holding the most important situations, as those of Viceroys, Governors of Subordinate Colonies, Archbishops, Deans, &c.; since, however, representatives of the colonies have been sent to the Cortes at Lisbon, Brahmins, Chardos, and even Sudras, have been admitted as candidates, and some have been elected. The Brahmins are the less numerous Indian caste, but much more numerous, indeed, than the two preceding put together.

The fourth class or caste is that of the *Chardos*, who, like the *Rajpoots* and *Parvos*, in other parts of India, pretend to be of the *Chatria*, or royal and military caste, (though many authors maintain that that caste, as well as that of the *Vaisias*, is now extinct.) This caste in the colony of Goa, is more numerous than that of the Brahmins, and held in equal estimation, though inferior with respect to rank.

The fifth class is that of the *Soodras* or *Sudras*, which, as in other parts of India, forms by far the greatest part of the population. In this colony, the Sudras are more numerous than all the other Christian inhabitants, both of the superior and inferior castes. They are not so much respected as the Brahmins and Chardos ; and formerly were not even admitted to holy orders, but that and all the other privileges of the two superior tribes, are now conceded to them, though they are not by far held in the same estimation.

The sixth class is that of the inferior Sudras, who follow the profession of fishermen and other viler occupations, called Corombis, Franzas, &c., and likewise the out-castes. They are similar to the *Parias* in the southern provinces of India, or to the coolies and other low castes in the north. They are, however, not treated with the same contempt as among the heathens; but they must remain in their own professions, and are not admitted to any place of trust whatsoever, which are held not only by the higher, but ordinary servants, who are all of the superior castes ; though reduced by poverty to serve, in order to gain their livelihood.

The slaves of Mosambique may be considered as the last Christian caste. They are employed like the preceding. As to the Pagan Hindoos, it would be foreign to the plan of this SKETCH, to enter into any details concerning them ; as their manners and distinctions of castes, are the same as those of the rest of Concan, which are sufficiently known from other English accounts.

The Mahometans, though generally every where throughout India, are in the proportion of one to ten Hindoos, are still in smaller proportion in this colony; there are besides them some few Parsees, chiefly at Pangi.

The members of the five superior tribes, very rarely marry out of their own castes, except the soldiers and some few Europeans of distinction, who may, but very rarely, enter into the bonds of matrimony with some descendants of pure European blood. It sometimes, however, happens that men of one caste take wives from the inferior ones, and the children in such cases retain the caste of their father; but never will a man of a superior caste, give his daughter in marriage to a man of an inferior one; and generally such mixed marriages take place between a man and a woman of the caste immediately following that of the man in inferiority. Except in regard to marriages, the five superior castes agree in most things; they make not the least difficulty of eating together, and of concurring in all the other circumstances of civil life; they likewise make no distinction of food whatsoever.

GOVERNMENT.

The supreme authority in the colony is vested in a chief magistrate, named by the King, and sent sometimes with the title of *Viceroy*, and sometimes with that of *Governor-General of Portuguese India*; he is always a nobleman, and his salary now amounts to near 20,000 Goa rupees per annum. The Viceroy or Governor, as representing the King, exercises an almost absolute power; the members of his council have only the power of advising him; he names to all the offices of the government and the army, and likewise of the Church, (except the deanery,) before the presentation of the Archbishop; and the latter names only, of his sole power, the assistants to the Vicars. In case of the death, or absence of the Viceroy or Governor, there are closed letters from Court always in readiness, which are then opened, and the persons therein named, administer as acting Governors; the first of these is generally the Archbishop, and the others, the officers civil and military, the most elevated in rank; they must always be Europeans.

The seat of government is now the palace of Pangi, wherein the governor resides and assembles his council, composed of the crown attorney, the commander-in-chief, the commandant of the sea and rivers, and the secretary-general. On the arrival of a new Viceroy or Governor, he is invested with the supreme administration, by his predecessor, or by the first of the acting governors, in one of the churches of Goa, generally in that of *Bom-Jesus.*

There are three courts of justice or tribunals in the colony, one in Margão for Salsette, one in Mapuça for Bardes, and the supreme tribunal, under the immediate jurisdiction of which are the island of Goa, and the other neighbouring smaller ones, is established at Ribandar, between Pangi and Pannely. This tribunal receives appeals from the two former, and has alone the power of judging capital criminal cases; the Viceroy or Governor, has the privilege of pardoning, commuting, or deferring the execution of a criminal in the King's name. These tribunals are composed of a chief judge and assistants called *Ouvidores*, or auditors; they are occasionally sent by the supreme tribunal of Ribandar to judge cases, occurring in the new provinces; these judges and *Ouvidores* are either Europeans or natives; the lawyers study at the two colleges or seminaries of Rachol and Chorão, or are instructed privately by other professional men, and are licensed to act by the Viceroy, after having been examined by a commission.

There is a collector for government residing in each of the provinces, and others are sent to collect revenues in the new ones.

The private concerns, and the police and internal administration of each of the three ancient provinces, are vested in the hands of three *Senates,* each composed of twelve senators, one of whom is president; that of Goa assembles in the city at the senate house, which we have described; and those of Salsette and of Bardes have their palaces or meeting places in Margão and Mapuça; they generally assemble but once a year.

There is besides a judge of the community in each of the three provinces, and there are two *Mestre dos Campos*, one in Salsette, and one in Bardes.

Each parish has a chief magistrate and a register.

Formerly there were three Regiments and a legion of Infantry in the colony ; at present there are eight Battalions, and a small company of Artillery, in the parish of St. Agnes, west of Pangi ; the whole amount to between 7 and 8,000 men, mostly natives, though, intermixed with many Europeans. Each battalion is commanded by a Colonel and there is a commander-in-chief, with the title of Field-Marshal, or *Mariscal de Campo* ; there is no Cavalry. Except the superior officers, all the others are indifferently Europeans or natives ; there are four forts, Aguada, Mormugao, Reis, opposite to Pangi, and Cabo.

RELIGION.

Little remains to be said upon this article, after the details we have already given in describing the city.

The mass of the population profess the Roman Catholic Religion. They are very regular in their attendance at church, and in the fulfilment of all their religious duties; the use of books in the churches for the laity is unknown; they assist at the church office, the men standing, kneeling, or sitting, on plain benches, and the women in the middle of the church, kneeling, or squatting upon their heels, with veils over their heads, rosaries in their hands, and with carpets under them, for such as can afford the same; both males and females are instructed, when young, in the Christian doctrine, previous to their taking their first Communion; and the men, as likewise those of the women who can read, are furnished at home with religious books. Sermons are preached on festivals and on Sundays of Advent and Lent.

The Catholics of Goa are all subject in spirituals to the Archbishop, who is named by the King and confirmed by the Pope, as the other prelates of the Portuguese dominions; he takes the title of *Primate of the East,* and as a Metropolitan, he has had, since the erection of his Archiepiscopal See, the seven following suffragan Bishoprics: Cochin, Malacca, Macao, Tunay, in Japan, Meliapoor, or St. Thomé, Nankin and Pekin, in China; that of Tunay never had but three Bishops, and is considered as extinct since the extermination of the Catholic religion in Japan; of the other Sees, only that of Macao, near Canton is regularly filled, and has a chapter of canons and dignitaries, who administer during the vacancies; those of Cochin, Meliapoor, and Malacca, are not filled regularly, and very often the titulars do not come to India, but continue to reside in Portugal, as it is still the King of that country who names them, and assigns them a revenue of 1,000 crusades per annum, though the episcopal towns are no longer under his temporal sway; as grand master of the order of Christ, the Pope has empowered him to name an Administrator or Vicar General, to administer the Sees when vacant, or when the titular has not taken possession thereof; this power he delegates to the Archhishop of Goa, who appoints regularly administrators for the dioceses of Cochin and Meliapoor; and likewise for the Archbishopric of Cranganor, erected in 1609, for the Catholic Christians of the Syrian rite, on the Malabar Coast; the administrators are simple priests, generally monks, and Europeans by birth or descent; they take the title of *Governadors*, or *Vicars-General*, *Acting Bishops*, *&c.* The See of Malacca, is generally administered by the Bishop of Macao; and as for those of Nankin and Pekin, they are always filled, when the titulars can penetrate into China. In case of vacancy in the Archiepiscopal See the Bishop of Cochin, (when that See is filled,) assumes the administration, by a special privilege from Rome; but when that See is likewise vacant, or the titular absent, the Archiepiscopal diocese is administered by the chapter.

The diocese of Goa is composed of the new and old provinces, the island of Angediva, and the government of Diu and Daman, all which are subject to Portugal, and likewise of the eighteen parishes of the island of Salsette, of two of that of Bombay, of eight on the mainland, around the abandoned city of Basseen, of several parishes or missions between Bombay and Goa, and of those of all the provinces of Canara, as far as Cannanore, where the diocese of Cranganor begins, and finally, of several other missions in the interior of the western part of India.

The number of secular priests in this diocese may amount to about 400; so that the greatest part are unemployed, and reside with their families: assisting voluntarily the Vicar of their native parish; the most populous parishes, however have regular assistants named by the Archbishop.

The Goa clergy are very poor, as has been seen, by the list I have already given of the revenues of the diverse benefices, or livings. They are in general most regular and exemplary in their manners, and the performance of their functions, by which it is evident that there must have been a very great reform among them, since near a century, if the accounts, which old travellers give, of the Goa priests of their times, be not false, or at least greatly exaggerated; they now all wear the clerical robe, or cassock, and the clerical cap, and are never seen out of their houses in any other dress.

They are far from being so ignorant as the English generally before them to be. They cannot, it is true, explain the Latin poets, and high prose writers, as well as it is done at Oxford and Cambridge, and many of them perhaps cannot do it at all; but they can all explain not only their office, their philosophy and divinity, and other Latin church books, but likewise, the easy authors, as Cornelius Nepos, &c, with perhaps more facility than Englishmen in general; and they have much more facility chiefly in talking, and few among them are incapable of keeping up conversation in Latin. If some Englishmen cannot understand them, it is entirely owing to their own way of pronouncing that language, which is unintelligible to all other European nations; as for one who pronounces the Latin after the French manner, (which I do not, however, pretend to be the true pronunciation, no more than that of the Portuguese), he understands them perfectly. I have always been able to converse with all the Goa priests that I have found and we have always understood each other perfectly well; there is not the least possible doubt, that it would be the same case, if they had to speak Latin with Spaniards, Italians, Germans, and even Scotchmen. Besides the Latin language, they all possess a perfect grammatical knowledge of the Portuguese, and an acquaintance with the country language, and are able to preach in both with equal ease; they know their philosophy and divinity, as well in general, as the mass of the French clergy; who have of all Catholic clergymen, been those who have escaped the reproach of ignorance, even from their enemies. But it must be owned that in history, geography, and the sciences, they are generally deficient, and know very little of the manners of other countries. As it is to be wished, on the one hand, that they should retain their honesty and simplicity of manners, and stick firmly to all their good habits, it should be likewise desirable on the other that they should study a little history, and the manners of other nations, which would divest them of many prejudices, and persuade them that many usages may be equally good, and, perhaps, better than those of Goa, and thus render them much more interesting in society. This would also have the good effect of clearing them in the eyes of foreigners, of the accusation of total ignorance, which they are too often, but most unjustly taxed with.

We have already sufficiently spoken of the monks, or regular clergy.

LANGUAGE AND EDUCATION.

The pure Portuguese language is spoken and known grammatically by all the clergy, the lawyers, physicians, magistrates, and all who can afford to receive any kind of education; all speak likewise a corrupt dialect, formed of the Portuguese, and the Concanee, or Mahratta language, which has been, however, reduced to grammatical rules; the poorest, and those who cannot read, chiefly the women, speak only this language. The Hindoostanee and other languages of India, are very little known in the colony. The priests, lawyers, and magistrates, generally understand French, sufficient to read all prose books in that language, but few can speak it. Many of the medical men and writers in the offices, understand English also, and some speak it; chiefly since the augmentation of intercourse with Bombay.

There is a school for boys established in every parish, in which are taught reading, writing and cyphering; in each of the three old provinces, are two masters of Latin grammar, appointed by the Governor; the two colleges, or seminaries, of Rachol and Chorao, are opened for the youth, who aspire to all professions; and they may there learn the Latin language, philosophy, and the canonical laws.

The young men who aspire to the medical profession, study either in the Royal hospital of Pannely, or with professed medical men; they are licenced by the Governor, after a due examination, like the Lawyers; the best physicians of Goa have of late admitted, in a great part, the English system of medicine; but there are ignorant native healers as all over India; and as for the other sciences there are only some few private teachers.

The education of the girls is rather deficient; a few are instructed in reading and writing at the nunnery of St. Monica, but the greatest part of those, whose parents can afford it, are instructed in their families by private tutors.

AGRICULTURE.

Rice being the most common food of the Goanese, it is likewise the chief object of agriculture; formerly, the colony did not produce sufficient for home consumption, but by the encouragement which the present Governor has given to that culture, chiefly in the new province of Ponda, there is now more than required, and sufficient even for exportation; next to rice, the culture of the cocoanut is the chief object of attention with the Goanese, as they make oil with it, and use the water thereof in almost all their dishes; this is the chief article of exportation, which is generally made to Bombay in the boats called pattimars, so well known in that presidency; they also export some salt. Though the high and rich classes eat bread, and the poor use flour for different kinds of cakes, yet, the country does not furnish wheat sufficient, and consequently a part must be imported; the mangoes of Goa, are, indeed, excellent, but, except to plantains, very little attention is paid to the culture of fruits, as likewise to vegetables, of which they are not very fond; the Indian corn, millet, and maguire, are only cultivated as curiosities and dainties. The *sura* or *toddy*, fermented and distilled into liquor, is the only common drink of the majority of the inhabitants, besides water.

The pasture is very good for the kine kind and the buffaloe, but not for sheep.

ANIMALS.

The animal flesh, more commonly eaten, is pork, fowl, and turkey, which are cheap and abundant; beef is likewise had at a low rate, but is rarely to be found for want of demand, except in the three chief towns, and on the table of the richest families; sheep and goat are rare; the wild animals in the colony are the tiger, the monkey, and the jackall, and all the reptiles of India, but there are no elephants, horses, camels, and asses, are never used, and are not to be found.

MANUFACTURES.

This article is entirely reduced to the making of shoes and clothes, by tailors; and the knitting of stockings by women; every other article and all sorts of cloth must be imported; so that clothing, crockery, and cutlery, are comparatively the dearest objects in Goa. There are carpenters and masons.

REVENUES.

The revenues of this colony are very small, and I have not been able to appreciate them even approximately, but this I have been informed of by competent authorities, namely, that the colony now suffices for all its expenses, and no money is sent from Portugal for the payment of the civil and military officers of Government, or for the clergy, or any other expenses whatever. As all the Goanese, in general, make a great use of tobacco, both for smoking and snuffing, the duties on that article amount to about 200,000 rupees, which form a part of the private revenue of the Queen of Portugal; this is the only profit which the mother country now reaps from this colony.

COMMERCE.

Except the pattimar trade of cocoanut and a little salt with Bombay, commerce is almost null. A ship or two generally come from Portugal yearly, but Brasil, Macao, or even Daman, as likewise Bombay and Surat, are more generally the chief objects of their voyage. One or two go from Goa to Macao, but generally touch first at Daman to take in opium. Daman is now not only comparatively, but really, more commercial than Goa; the customhouse is established at present at Pangi, and very few vessels go up the city, unless it be to load some articles from the arsenal.

GENERAL OBSERVATIONS ON THE MANNERS OF THE GOANESE.

All the ancient travellers expatiate, with what justice it is not easy to ascertain, on the corruption of manners of the inhabitants of Goa, on the profligacy and jealousy of the men, the no less immorality of the women, the frequency of murders, &c. It is certain that the authors of the life of St. Francis Xavier themselves, though Portuguese, give a dreadful account of the state of morals in Goa, at the arrival of that celebrated missionary, who, however, in a little time, operated a thorough change for the better, but matters may have afterwards again retaken their old way ; yet, howsoever they may have been in the flourishing state of this settlement, it would be very unjust and contrary to truth, to think, that there are still remains of that ancient corruption of manners. On the contrary it would be difficult to find a community of the same number of individuals, pursuing a more regular, tranquil and moral conduct, than that of the present inhabitants of Goa ; very seldom, indeed, does there happen any misconduct among the females, not only of the first respectability, but of the great majority of the population. If some of the young men behave, as too many of other countries do, and which is difficult to suppose never to be the case in any place, they at least take great care to conceal the disorder in their conduct; quarrels are very rare, and murders, or even duels are still more so ; the least regulated in their demeanours are the European soldiers who settle in the colony ; except these and a few others, chiefly Europeans, I have been well assured that all, without exception, perform their annual confessions and receive their Easter Communions, a circumstance, which, whatever others may think of it, I have found in all the Catholic countries I have been in, to be a very great, if not, an absolute proof of the rest of the private conduct of the people being as it should be.

There are very few rich families in this colony, and no fortune exceeds an annual income of 20,000 rupees. If there be two or three amounting to what it is all that can be expected, all the others fall far short of it, and the vast majority, even of those accounted considerable, do not exceed two thousand rupees ; those of one thousand are still more numerous ; and the income of those families, who are deemed in easy circumstances, though not rich, amount to between five hundred and six hundred rupees. It is supposed that a quarter of a rupee, or half *Pardao*, is sufficient for the decent maintenance of a single individual ; but fourfifths at least of the population are truly poor and miserable. Hence, as it is well known, a great part of all the castes, exercise the functions of servants, for which, many receive only one rupee, or at most two or three rupees a month. Many now go to Bombay, and to other parts of the Presidency where they find the exercise of their professions more profitable ; the cooks, chiefly of all the Europeans and easy inhabitants at the Presidency, are almost all natives of Goa ; they, however, seldom go to Bengal, Madras, or the Eastern Coast in order to keep near their native land, as much as possible they return to, visit it, some every year, some less often ; many even marry in Goa, leaving their wives in the houses of their fathers-in-law, going every now then to see them, and bringing them a part of the fruit of their labour ; some, who are fortunate enough, find situations in Bombay, and other stations of that part of India, as writers, and guardians of the sick in the hospitals.

The families, who remain in the colony, are given up to agriculture, or live upon their rents; there are a pretty good number exercising the profession of lawyers, and physicians; some are shop-keepers in the towns, but there are hardly any regular merchants. In every family, that can afford it, one of the boys at least, takes to the church, from indolence, which is perhaps the greatest reproach that can now be cast on the Goanese.

All the men wear the European dress, and use their black coats, much oftener than many British residents in India. It is sometimes very odd to see, in the middling class, men with cloth coats, waistcoats, short breeches, and shoes, without stockings. The poorest of the men, except the slaves, wear a shirt, jacket, and breeches, without hats or shoes. The women, in rich and easy circumstances, dress after the actual European fashion; some also of the latter, use the old Portuguese dress, consisting of a plain linen cap, long waistcoats, thick silk striped petticoats, made of those stuffs which are manufactured throughout Guzerat, and large and thick black veils over their heads, when they go out. The poorer class are dressed, like the Mahratta Christian women, of the islands of Bombay and Salsette, which does not much differ from that of the Indians, having rings, or bracelets in their ankles and wrists, and part of their legs bare. When they go to church, they wrap themselves up in a large piece of white linen as a veil and overall.

The food of the poorer sort, consists chiefly in rice, fish, plantains, other fruits, and some cakes of flour; they do not eat meat more than three or four times a year; they season their dishes with ghee, or clarified butter, after the manner of the Indians; curry is their principal dish, and rice congee is their only morning and evening meal; cocoanut water enters in almost every thing they eat.

Rich and easy families take their breakfast between seven and eight, after hearing Mass; it now chiefly consists of tea, bread, and butter, and sometimes coffee; some, however, keep to the old way of eating rice congee; between twelve and one, dinner is taken. The richest have soup, and boiled and roast meat, and always finish by rice and curry before the desert, which consists of cakes and sweetmeats; they drink Madeira, Lisbon and other Portuguese wines; those less easy take no soup, but never omit the curry, and they drink *urraca*; they have a particular way of dressing rice, which is very much like the Turkish pilow; the use of sleeping after dinner is universal. At four they drink plain tea, some adding cakes and biscuits; the supper is taken at eight, and chiefly consists of fish curry and rice; very few eat flesh meat; they are all in general very fond of smoking, and many even among the women.

The only kind of conveyances for the rich, are palkies, or rather covered manchils and boats; as navigation can be carried on to almost every part of the colony, by means of the numerous rivers and streams.

Their only amusements consist in visits, playing at cards, and sometimes drafts and balls; the other great rendezvous, takes place only at church, on religious festivals. After the morning service, a small fair is held near the door of the church, consisting of articles of crockery, cutlery, small looking glasses, rosaries, sweetmeats and cakes; in every family there is on that day, a more plentiful and ceremonious meal.

These are the informations which I have been able to collect, concerning the history and present state of the colony of Goa. Though my first intention, in undertaking this little work, was to have it published in Europe, other considerations have determined me to commit it to the press in India; and one of the chief reasons, is the hope that persons, well informed on the subject, may be kind enough to favor me with their observations, which shall indeed be faithfully, and thankfully attended to, and inserted in a second Edition, provided I succeed in acquiring the approbation of the generality of my readers, by the first.

FINIS.

A FIGURATIVE PLAN OF THE CITY OF GOA.

Taken on the Spot, comprehending a Space of Ground of about one mile and a half from East to West and three-quarters of a mile from North to South.

[Churches in good repair are not shaded, but have crosses marking the altars. Convents and other buildings in good repair are shaded dark. Churches and other buildings in ruins are shaded round the edges only.]

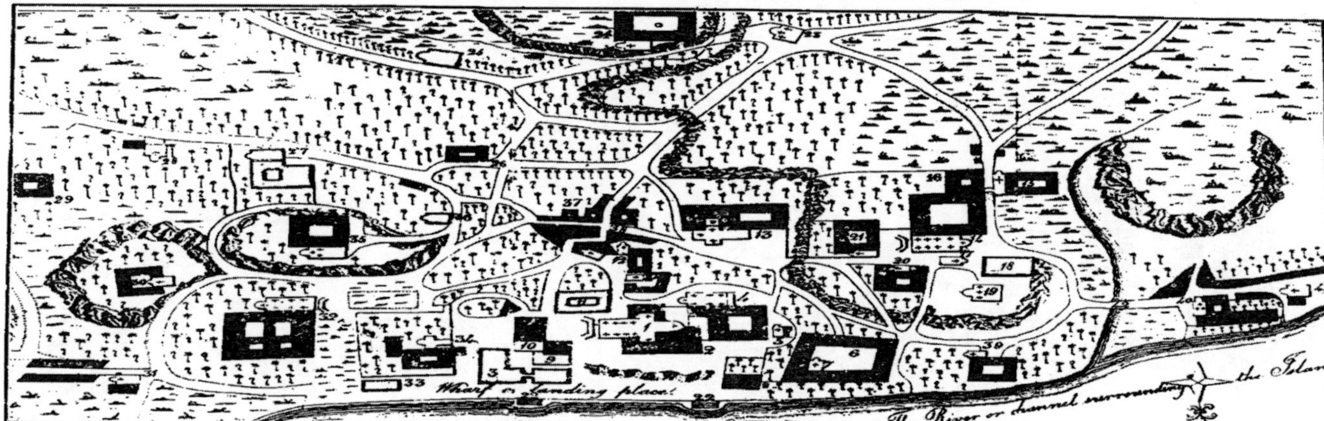

References and Explanations.

1 Cathedral.
2 Archiepiscopal palace.
3 Palace of the Viceroy in ruins.
4 Church and Convent of St. Francis.
5 Chapel of St. Catherine.
6 Arsenal.
7 Chapel of the 5 Wounds in the Arsenal
8 Archbishop's Prison or Aljuvar.
9 Senate House.
10 Old Senate House, now an hospital.
11 Inquisition in ruins.
12 3 Churches & houses of Misericordia.
13 Church and House of Bom Jesus, with the shrine of St. Francis Xavier.
14 Church & convent of St. Augustine.
15 College of the Augustinians.
16 Novitiate of the same.
17 Chapel of St. Antony of Padua.
18 College of St. Rock in ruins.
19 Collegiate and parochial church of the Rosary.
20 Nunnery of St. Monica.
21 Convent & church of St. John of God.
22 Landing Stairs.
23 Collegiate & parochial church of Luz.
24 Church of the Miraculous Cross belonging to and adjoining the convent of the priests of the Congregation.
25 Parochl. church of the Bd. Trinity in ruins.
26 Old City Hospital almost abandoned.
27 Ch. and college of St. Paul in ruins.
28 Parochial ch. of St. Thomas Ap.
29 Hospital of St. Lazarus.
30 Church and house of N. Senhora del Monte.
31 Parochial church of St. Lucia.
32 Church and Convent of St. Dominic.
33 Old Custom house in ruins.
34 Church and Convent of St. Cajetan.
35 Anot. ch. and convent of the Carmelites now col. of the priests of the Congr.
36 Parochl. ch. of St. Alexius in ruins.
37 Slaughter house.
38 Bazar.
39 College of St. Bonaventure belg. to the Order of the Franciscans.
40 College of St. Thomas Aquinas belonging to the Dominicans in the suburb of Pannely.
41 Parochial Church of St. Peter in the suburb of Pannely.
42 Bridge over the ditch, the waters of which flow from the hills.